BADMINTON

SCOTT, FORESMAN PHYSICAL ACTIVITIES SERIES
EDITED BY J. TILLMAN HALL

BADMINTON

JAMES POOLE
California State University, Dominguez Hills

3RD EDITION

Scott, Foresman and Company
Glenview, Illinois

Dallas, Tex.   Oakland, N.J.   Palo Alto, Cal.   Tucker, Ga.   London, England

Library of Congress Cataloging in Publication Data

Poole, James.
  Badminton.

  (Scott, Foresman physical activities series)
  1. Badminton (Game) I. Title. II. Series
GV1007.P6   1982   796.34′5   81-18387
ISBN 0-673-16041-6   AACR2

BADMINTON

Third Edition

James Poole
ISBN: 0-673-16041-6

Copyright © 1982, 1973, 1969
Scott, Foresman and Company.
All Rights Reserved.
Printed in the United States of America.

   2 3 4 5 6 7 8-KPF-88 87 86 85 84 83

ACKNOWLEDGMENTS

I would like to thank Herbert Scheele of England, who assisted in the area of history and gave permission as secretary of the International Badminton Federation to reprint the laws of badminton. I also deeply thank David Ogata and Ken Purdy for the photography and also all of the American players who allowed their photographs to be used in this book. Finally, my deepest thanks to Dr. George Ziegenfuss and Carl Loveday who gave me inspiration and encouragement in my younger days of competition in badminton and other sports.

CONTENTS

EDITOR'S NOTE

Scott, Foresman and Company presents a series of physical education books written by instructors expert in their respective fields.

These books on major sports are intended as supplementary material for the instructor and to aid the student in the understanding and mastery of the sport of his or her choice. Each book covers its fundamentals—the beginning techniques, rules and customs, equipment and terms—and gives to the reader the spirit of the sport.

Each author of this series brings to the reader the knowledge and skill acquired over many years of teaching and coaching. We sincerely hope that these books will prove invaluable to the college student or any student of the sport.

In BADMINTON, James Poole presents the history, terms, equipment, fundamental to advanced skills, and strategy of this popular game. From his experience at Louisiana State University, California State University, Northridge, California State University, Dominguez Hills, and as the men's singles champion in the United States, James Poole is able to bring the student a comprehensive analysis of badminton. Since 1958, James Poole has won 36 national championships.

This book reveals the early history of badminton and describes its development from the courts of England to the gymnasiums of the United States. The author has included many line drawings and photographs that clearly illustrate all foot, hand, and body positions essential to master the game. He also includes a set of self-testing standards by which the student can evaluate his progress as he acquires the basic techniques. Court specifications, and the rules and their interpretations are also covered. Badminton is a sport that is still growing in popularity; it is quick, challenging, and fun.

HISTORY

The origin of badminton is somewhat cloudy; documents show evidence of the game having been played in several countries. A version of badminton in China used wooden paddles and a ball. There is some mention of the game as far back as the twelfth century in the royal court records of England. There is also evidence that a member of the royal family of Poland played it in the late seventeenth or early eighteenth centuries. In India it was played at Poona, and called by that name for some time in the 1870s. It has not been clearly established whether English army officers took the game to India or brought it to England from India. What is definitely known is that the name *badminton* comes from the town of Badminton, home of the Duke of Beaufort.

Mr. H.A.E. Scheele, former secretary of the

International Badminton Federation (IBF), offered the following information about the origin of the game:

> . . . I would say that to the best of my knowledge it is quite clear that the game was first played at the home of the Duke of Beaufort which is situated in a town called Badminton in Gloucestershire, which is not very far from Bristol. There is even some uncertainty as to the date of the invention. One or two books written many years ago have given certain dates of about 1870, but the present Duke told me himself a few years ago that he was quite convinced that the date must have been 3–4 years earlier than that.
>
> Where the first club was is also quite a mystery, and this is not particularly surprising. In the old days of about 100 years ago such things as clubs did not exist for anything as they do now, and the game will have been restricted altogether in early years to being played in the enormous drawing room possessed by the aristocracy. However, I have always understood that Folkestone did form the first club, though I may be biased in being guilty of wishful thinking because Folkestone is in my own county of Kent.
>
> There exists nothing in the way of printed historical information and the earliest book written on the game was not published until 1911. This was a book called *Badminton* by S. M. Massey, a well-known player early in the century and a man of some importance at the time in the administration, such as it was, of the game.

The original rules of the game were drawn up in 1877, revised in 1887, and again in 1890. The present rules of the IBF differ only slightly from the 1890 draft.

Prior to 1901, when the present court dimensions and shape were adopted, courts varied considerably, although most were of the hourglass shape. This shape can be traced back to the Duke of Beaufort's room in which badminton was played. Two doors opened inwards on the side walls near the net area, and it was decided to narrow the court at the net in order to allow nonplayers to enter and leave the room without disturbing play, hence the hourglass shaped court. As for the size of the court, one at Ealing in West London measured 60′ by 30′, and it is believed that local players on this court had some advantage over their visitors in matches. It was quite common to play three to four to a side in those days, while singles matches were unknown.

The first All-England championships were held in 1897 and were completed in one day, in contrast to the elaborate arrangements and four days now required to finish the meeting. The success of this first meeting served as a great impetus to the game throughout the British Isles.

The Badminton Union of Ireland was founded in 1889 and promoted its first championship in 1902. The first international match between England and Ireland was played in 1903. The Scottish championships were first played at Aberdeen in 1907, and the union was formed in 1911. *The Badminton Gazette*, which is still the official journal of the Badminton Association of England, was founded in 1907 and is now nearing its fiftieth volume.

These early tournaments did much to encourage the game and were very popular with the players. Players from other countries came to England to play and to learn the game, and teams played matches in Europe. In 1925 and 1930 an English team toured Canada, and influenced the increase of badminton in the United States and Canada. The Canadian Badminton Association was formed in 1931, and the American Badminton Association (ABA) in 1936. The founding of the International Badminton Federation in 1934 helped to foster international play. Sir George Thomas, a famous English player and administrator of the game, presented the Thomas Cup (run on almost identical lines as tennis's Davis Cup) to be challenged for by members of the IBF. After a setback caused by the outbreak of war in 1939, the first International Competition for the Thomas Cup was inaugurated in 1948–49. Ten countries playing in three zones competed in the first competition, which resulted in a win for Malaysia, whose team beat Denmark in the finals at Preston, England, in February, 1949. This competition is held every three years.

In 1950, Mrs. H. S. Uber, still considered by many to be the finest woman mixed doubles player the game has ever known, felt it was time that women be included in international competition. She donated the magnificent trophy bearing her name, and the Ladies International Badminton Championship, for Uber Cup competition, was born. The first competition for the cup was played in 1957; subsequent competitions are at three-year intervals. The three first competitions were won by the United States.

For the most part, the top players in the world come from the Far East. Perhaps the reason is that badminton is considered the national game in Malaysia, Indonesia, and Thailand and a player is treated as we in the United States would treat a football or baseball hero. The tournaments and Thomas Cup competitions in Djakarta and Singapore will play before 10 to 25 thousand spectators. The Malaysians and Indonesians have dominated the Thomas Cup team competitions since its inception in 1949. Japan and Indonesia have dominated the Uber Cup team competitions since the United States last won in 1965.

Until recently, the individual winners of the All-England Championships were considered the world champions and many feel that this is still true, although there has been a world championship tournament the last two years. Some of the outstanding international players in recent years are: Judy Devlin Hashman of the United States and England (seventeen All-England titles in singles and doubles), Finn Kobboro of Denmark (fifteen All-England titles in doubles and mixed), Erland Kops of Denmark (eleven All-England titles in singles and doubles), Rudy Hartono of Indonesia (eight All-England titles in singles—seven in a row which is a record), Gillian Gilks of England (eight All-England titles in singles, doubles, and mixed), and the Indonesian men's doubles team of Tjun Tjun and Wahjudi (six All-England titles—the last four in a row).

A new country will undoubtedly be heard from in the future as Red China is now playing (and winning) exhibition matches against the world champion Indonesians and other Far East countries.

The first American championships were held in 1937 in Chicago, with Walter Kramer of Detroit winning the men's singles and Mrs. Dell Barkuff of Seattle the women's singles. Since then (except for the war years during the forties, when it wasn't played) the United States Nationals has been held in different cities throughout the country. Starting in 1954, the United States Nationals became an "open" championship which allowed foreigners to compete. The open nationals was advocated by many officials in hopes of improving the quality of American play. In 1970, the United States Nationals went to a "closed" and "open" championships. Only American residents are eligible to play in the closed with selected Americans and all foreign players eligible for the open events. The American Badminton Association changed its name to the U.S. Badminton Association in 1976.

The United States has never won the Thomas Cup, but has won the Uber Cup on three occasions. Even though we might not be among the best in international play, it is interesting that perhaps the top man and woman players of all time come from the United States. Dr. David G. Freeman maintained an amazing record of not having been defeated in singles play from 1939 until 1953, when he finally retired, beating the best players in the world in 1949 when he met them in Thomas Cup and All-England play. Judy Devlin Hashman has won over 31 United States national titles and 17 All-England titles since 1954. She officially retired from singles play in 1967 after winning her tenth world singles title.

OPEN BADMINTON

In the past year, international badminton has moved toward "open play" with players having the option of remaining amateurs or being *licensed*. The licensed player will be able to accept money prizes while amateurs

must accept trophies or the maximum of 500 Swiss
Francs per event. The first open tournament of any
consequence was held last year in London and called
the Friends Provident Masters Tournament. It awarded
$40,000 in prize money to the participants. Denmark
followed with the Randers Open that also awarded
considerable prize money and was sponsored by a bank.
Television showed both the Friends and Randers
tourneys and most believe it came off well in both
countries. Also, for the first time, the United States
championships held in April 1980 awarded prize money.
General Sportcraft Sporting Goods Company donated
$5,000 for prizes. The money was limited, but it is a
beginning, which most players hope will bring higher
amounts of prize money and more exposure of

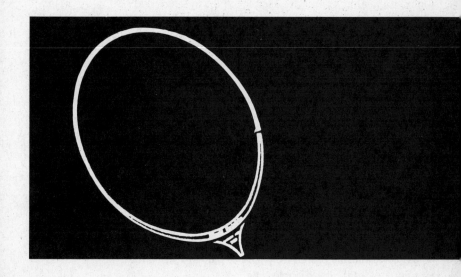

badminton to the people of the United States.

In most countries of the world the only players who work full-time in badminton are teaching professionals or administrative personnel such as executive secretaries of national associations, etc. Currently, the United States has only one person who is teaching professionally full-time in badminton and there is no one getting paid as an administrator on the local or national level. There are a few players in the world who now train and play badminton as their full-time job and make a decent living from it. There are approximately eight players in England who earn about $40,000 a year from prize money and product endorsements. Denmark and Sweden also have a few players earning a living from playing badminton, so the era of professional badminton players has begun.

2

TERMINOLOGY

Alley

The 1½′ extension on both sides of the court used in doubles play.

Attacking Clear

A shot hit to barely clear the racket of an opponent and carry to the back of opponent's court. Sometimes called an "offensive clear."

Back Alley

Area between the back boundary line and the long service line in doubles. This area is 2½′ in depth.

Backcourt

The back half of the court in the general area of the back boundary lines.

Backhand

The nonracket side of the body. For right-handed players it would be the left side of the body and includes all strokes made on this side.

Baseline

The lines parallel to the net which limit the playing area at the end boundaries of the court.

Base

The spot approximately in the center of the court to which a player tries to return after each shot.

Bird

A commonly used term for the shuttle, the missile used in place of a ball.

Block

Placing the racket in front of the shuttle and letting it rebound off the racket to the opponent's side of the court. Very little stroke is made.

Carry

Holding the shuttle on the racket during the execution of a stroke. This is an illegal shot. Usually the shuttle will leave the racket in a direction different than the player intended to hit it.

Clear (or Lob)

A high, deep shot hit to the back of the opponent's court.

Combination Doubles Formation

A combination of the side-by-side and up-and-back formations. Explained more fully in Chapter 9.

Court

Area of play. Although the size varied during the 1800s, it has been standardized since the 1930s. It is 20' by 44' for doubles and 17' by 44' for singles.

Cross-Court

A stroke hit diagonally from one side of the court to the other.

Deception

Deceiving one's opponent by changing the direction and speed of the shuttle at the last second.

Double Hit

Hitting the shuttle twice in succession on the same stroke. This is illegal.

Drive

A hard, flat shot which makes a horizontal flight across the net. Usually hit close to the net as it crosses and downward when possible.

Drive Serve

A hard, quick serve with a flat trajectory. Usually used in doubles and aimed at the opponent's head or left shoulder.

Drop

A stroke which just clears the net and immediately starts to fall in the opponent's court.

Fault

A violation of the rules. Faults can be during service, by both server or receiver, or during play.

First Service

A term used in doubles to indicate that the team still has both its serves.

Flick Serve

Used in doubles when your opponent is expecting a low serve. A quick wrist and forearm rotation changes a soft shot into a faster passing shot.

Foot Fault

A violation of the rules in which the feet of the server, or receiver, are not in the position required by the laws. This could be illegal position and/or movement.

Forecourt

This is the area of the court nearest the net; usually refers to the area between the net and the short service line.

Forehand

The racket side of the body. For right-handed players it would be the right side of the body and includes all strokes made on this side.

Game

The unit of points necessary to win the game. Fifteen points in men's singles and in all doubles constitutes a game; eleven points constitutes a game in women's singles. (See *Setting*.)

Game Bird

The point that will enable the server to win the game.

Hairpin Net Shot

Stroke made from below and close to the net with the shuttle rising and just clearing the net to fall sharply downward on the opposite side. Name is taken from the path of the shuttle's flight.

Half-Court Shot

A shot played to midcourt, usually low, used in doubles and mixed doubles against up-and-back formations.

Hand-In

Term used to show that the player serving still retains the service.

Hand-Out

Term used to show that one player in doubles has lost the service.

IBF

International Badminton Federation, the world governing body founded in 1934.

Inning

The terms of service. Time during which a player or team holds the service.

Kill

A fast, downward return which usually cannot be returned.

Let

A legitimate stoppage of play due to interference from outside the court. It can also be called after a rally if a player or team served to received in the wrong court (depending on who wins the rally). It is replayed. (Refer to Laws 12 and 17.)

Love

A term used to indicate no score. If the score is "3–love," it means the server has three and the opponent has zero. Umpire usually starts singles games by calling "Love–all, play."

Love–All

A term which indicates the score is 0–0. It is also used when a game has been set. (See *Setting*.)

Match ✓
A match is usually best two out of three games.

Match Point
The point which, if won by the server, wins the match.

Midcourt
The center of the court area approximately halfway between the net and the back boundary line.

Net Shot ✓
A shot played in the forecourt that barely clears the net and then drops rapidly.

Obstruction ✓
When a player hinders an opponent from playing the shot. Usually called if a player who hits a poor net shot holds the racket up at the net and disconcerts the opponent, who is trying to kill this poor shot.

Overhead
A stroke played above head height.

Passing Shot
A shot that goes past an opponent to the side, as contrasted to one going over the head.

Pronation
An inward turning of the wrist and forearm which is used in all overhead forehand strokes requiring power.

Racket (or Racquet)
The implement used in the hand to hit the shuttle.

Rally
The exchange of strokes back and forth while the shuttle is in play until it becomes dead.

Ready Position
The alert position that the player assumes just before the opponent strokes the shuttle. It is usually with slightly flexed knees and racket held about chest high.

Receiver
The player who receives the service.

Round-the-Head-Shot

A forehand stroke made on the backhand side of the body. Usually hit overhead and can be either a clear, drop, or smash.

Rush the Serve

Quick move to the net by the receiver after the serve has been struck to put away a low serve that is weak. Used mostly in doubles and mixed doubles play.

Second Service

A term used in doubles play to indicate that one person has lost the service and is "down," the partner still retains the serve.

Serve or Service

The act of putting the shuttle into play by hitting it into the opponent's court.

Server

The player who delivers the service.

Service Court

The area into which the serve must be delivered. This area will depend on whether singles or doubles is played, and also depends on the score.

Setting

The method of extending the game by playing additional points when the score is tied at specific scores in a game. The player or team reaching this score first has the option of setting.

Short Service Line

The line 6½' from the net that serves must cross to be legal.

Shuttlecock

The official name for the shuttle or bird. The shuttles today are of two types: (1) goose feathers, and (2) nylon.

Side In

This terms refers to the side whose turn it is to serve.

Side Out

This occurs when the side that is serving loses the serve and becomes the receiving team.

Side-by-Side Formation

A doubles formation used in either regular doubles or mixed doubles.

Sling or Throw

The term to indicate that the shuttle was carried by the racket. It is illegal.

Smash ✓

The hard overhead stroke hit downward with great force. It is the principal attacking stroke in badminton.

Stroke

The action of striking the shuttle with the racket.

Supination

An outward turning of the wrist and forearm which is used in all overhead backhand strokes which require power.

Underhand ✓

A stroke which is made when the shuttle is contacted below the level of the shoulders. It usually refers to a shot being hit upward.

Unsight

When the partner of the server stands in such a position that the receiver cannot see the serve being struck. This is illegal.

Up-and-Back Formation

A doubles and mixed doubles formation. The predominant formation that is used in mixed.

USBA ✓

United States Badminton Association, national governing body in the United States since 1976 (formerly called ABA, from 1936 to 1976).

Wood Shot

The shot which results when the shuttle is struck by the frame of the racket. A legal shot under present rules.

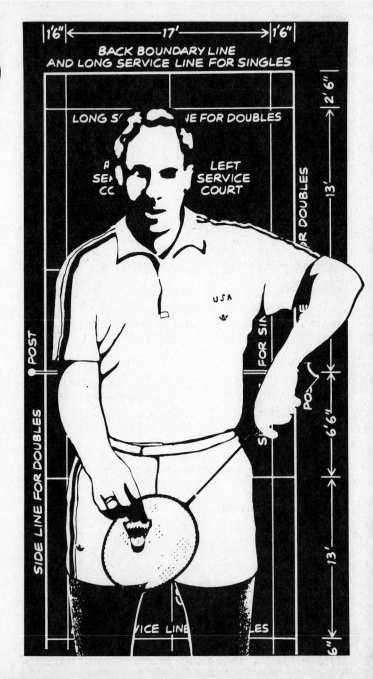

Read

THE LAWS OF BADMINTON

ULES

Rule 1

Court

(a) The court shall be laid out as shown in Figure 3.1A
(except in the case provided for in paragraph (b) of
the Law) and to the measurements there shown, and
shall be defined by white, black or other easily
distinguishable lines, 1½" wide.

In marking the court, the width (1½") of the center
lines shall be equally divided between the right and
left service courts; the width (1½" each) of the short
service line and the long service line shall fall within
the 13' measurement given as the length of
the service court; and the width (1½" each) of all
other boundary lines shall fall within the
measurements given.

Reprinted with permission of the International Badminton Federation.

(b) Where space does not permit the marking out of a court for doubles, a court may be marked for singles only as shown in Figure 3.1B. The back boundary lines also become the long service lines, and the posts, or the strips of materials representing them as referred to in Law 2, shall be placed on the side lines.

Rule 2

Posts. The posts shall be 5'1" in height from the surface of the court. They shall be sufficiently firm to keep

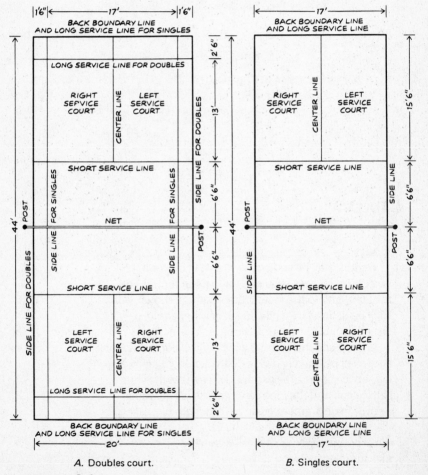

A. Doubles court.   *B.* Singles court.

Figure 3.1

the net strained as provided in Law 3, and shall be placed on the side boundary lines of the court. Where this is not practicable, some method must be employed for indicating the position of the side boundary line where it passes under the net, e.g., by the use of a thin post or strip of material, not less than 1½″ in width, fixed to the side boundary line and rising vertically to the net cord. Where this is in use on a court marked for doubles it shall be placed on the side boundary line of the doubles court regardless of whether singles or doubles is being played.

Rule 3

Net. The net shall be made of fine natural cord or artificial fibre of a dark colour and an even thickness not less than ⅝″ and not more than ¾″ mesh. It shall be firmly stretched from post to post, and shall be 2′6″ in depth. The top of the net shall be 5′ in height from the floor at the center, and 5′1″ at the posts, and shall be edged with a 3″ white tape doubled and supported by a cord or cable run through the tape and strained over and flush with the top of the posts.

Rule 4

Shuttle

(a) A shuttle shall have from 14 to 16 feathers fixed in a cork base which is 0.025 to 0.028 metres (1 inch to 1⅛ inches) in diameter. The feathers shall be from 0.064 to 0.070 metres (2½ to 2¾ inches) in length from the tip to the top of the cork base.

The tips of the feathers shall form a circle with a diameter within the range from 0.054 to 0.064 metres (2⅛ to 2½ inches). The feathers shall be fastened firmly with thread or other suitable material. The bottom of the cork shall be rounded and covered by a thin layer of white leather or similar material.

(b) Weight. A shuttle shall weigh from 73 to 85 grains (4.74 to 5.50 grammes).

(c) Pace and Flight. A shuttle shall be deemed to be of correct pace when it is hit by a player with a full underhand stroke from a spot immediately above one back boundary line in a direction parallel to the side lines and at an upward angle, to fall not less than 0.30 metres (1') and not more than 0.76 metres (2'6") short of the other back boundary line.

(d) Subject to there being no variation in the general design, weight, pace and flight of the shuttle, modifications in the above specifications may be made, with the approval of the national organization concerned:

    i) in places where atmospheric conditions due either to altitude or climate make the standard shuttle unsuitable; or

    ii) if special circumstances exist which make it otherwise necessary in the interests of the game.

Rule 5

Players

(a) The word "Player" applies to all those taking part in a game.

(b) The game shall be played, in the case of the doubles game, by two players a side, and in the case of the singles game, by one player a side.

(c) The side for the time being having the right to serve shall be called the "In" side, and the opposing side shall be called the "Out" side.

Rule 6

Toss. Before commencing play the opposing sides shall toss, and the side winning the toss shall have the option of:

(a) Serving first; or

(b) Not serving first; or

(c) Choosing ends.

The side losing the toss shall then have the choice of any alternative remaining.

Rule 7

Scoring

(a) The doubles and men's singles game consists of 15 points, provided that when the score is 13 all, the side which first reaches 13 has the option of "setting" the game to 5, and that when the score is 14 all, the side which first reaches 14 has the option of "setting" the game to 3. After a game has been "set" the score is called "love all," and the side which first scores 5 to 3 points, according as the game has been "set" at 13 all or 14 all, wins the game. In either case the claim to "set" the game must be made before the next service is delivered after the score has reached 13 all or 14 all.

(b) The women's singles game consists of 11 points. Provided that when the score is "9 all" the player who first reaches 9 has the option of "setting" the game to 3, and when the score is "10 all" the player who first reaches 10 has the option of "setting" the game to 2.

(c) A side rejecting the option of "setting" at the first opportunity shall not thereby be debarred from "setting" if a second opportunity arises.

(d) Notwithstanding paragraph (a) above, it is permissible by prior arrangement for only one game to be played and also for this to consist of 21 points, in which "setting" shall be as for the game of 15 points with scores of 19 and 20 being substituted for 13 and 14 respectively.

(e) In handicap games "setting" is not permitted.

Rule 8

The opposing sides shall contest the best of three games, unless otherwise agreed. The players shall change ends at the commencement of the second game and also of the third game (if any). In the third game the players shall change ends when the leading score reaches:

(a) 8 in a game of 15 points;

(b) 6 in a game of 11 points;

or, in handicap events, when one of the sides has scored half the total number of points required to win the game (the next highest number being taken in case of fractions). When it has been agreed to play only one game the players shall change ends as provided above for the third game. In a game of 21 points, the players shall change ends when the leading score reaches 11 or in handicap games as indicated above.

If, inadvertently, the players omit to change ends as provided in this Law at the score indicated, the ends shall be changed immediately the mistake is discovered, and the existing score shall stand.

Rule 9

Doubles Play

(a) It having been decided which side is to have the first service, the player in the right-hand service court of that side commences the game by serving to the player in the service court diagonally opposite. If the latter player returns the shuttle before it touches the ground, it is to be returned by one of the "In" side, and then returned by one of the "Out" side, and so on, till a fault is made or the shuttle ceases to be "in play" (see paragraph (b)). If a fault is made by the "In" side its right to continue serving is lost, as only one player on the side beginning a game is entitled to do so (see Law 11), and the opponent in the right-hand service court then becomes the server; but, if the service is not returned, or the fault is made by the "Out" side, the "In" side scores a point. The "In" side players then change from one service court to the other, the service now being from the left-hand service court to the player in the service court diagonally opposite. As long as a side remains "in," service is delivered alternately from each service court into the one diagonally opposite, the change being made by the "In" side when, and only when, a point is added to its score.

(b) The first service of a side in each inning shall be made from the right-hand service court. A "Service" is delivered as soon as the shuttle is struck by the server's racket. The shuttle is thereafter "in play" until it touches the ground, or until a fault or "let" occurs, or except as provided in Law 19. After the service is delivered the server and the player served to may take up any position they choose on their side of the net, irrespective of any boundary lines.

Rule 10

The player served to may alone receive the service, but should the shuttle touch, or be struck by, his partner the "In" side scores a point. No player may receive two consecutive services in the same game, except as provided in Law 12.

Rule 11

Only one player of the side beginning a game shall be entitled to serve in its first inning. In all subsequent innings each partner shall have the right, and they shall serve consecutively. The side winning a game shall always serve first in the next game, but either of the winners may serve and either of the losers may receive the service.

Rule 12

If a player serves out of turn, or from the wrong service court (owing to a mistake as to the service court from which service is at the time being in order), *and his or her side wins the rally*, it shall be a "Let," provided that such "Let" be claimed and allowed or ordered by the umpire before the next succeeding service is delivered.

If a player of the "Out" side standing in the wrong service court is prepared to receive the service when it is delivered, and his side wins the rally, it shall be a "Let," provided that such "Let" be claimed and allowed, or ordered by the umpire, before the next succeeding service is delivered.

If in either of the above cases the side at fault *loses the rally*, the mistake shall stand and the players' positions shall not be corrected during the remainder of the game.

Should a player inadvertently change sides when he should not do so, and the mistake not be discovered until after the next succeeding service has been delivered, the mistake shall stand, and a "Let" cannot be claimed or allowed, and the player's position shall not be corrected during the remainder of that game.

Rule 13

Singles Play. In singles Law 9 to 12 hold good except that:
(a) The players shall serve from and receive in their respective right-hand service courts only when the server's score is 0 or an even number of points in the game, the service being delivered from and received

in their respective left-hand service courts when the server's score is an odd number of points. Setting does not affect this sequence.

(b) Both players shall change service courts after each point has been scored.

Rule 14

Faults. A fault made by a player of the side which is "In," puts the server out; if made by a player whose side is "Out," it counts a point to the "In" side.

It is a fault:

(a) If in serving, (i) any part of the shuttle at the instant of being struck is higher than the server's waist, or (ii) if at the instant of the shuttle being struck the shaft of the racket is not pointing in a downward direction to such an extent that the whole of the head of the racket is discernibly below the whole of the server's hand holding the racket. See Figure 3.2

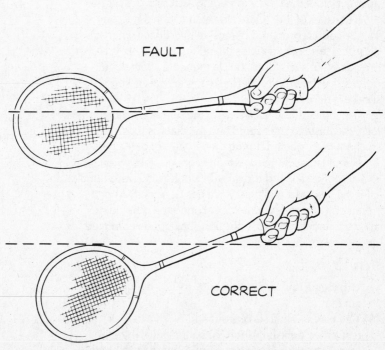

FAULT

CORRECT

Figure 3.2 *Legal and illegal racket head positions.*

(b) If, in serving, the shuttle does not pass over the net, or falls into the wrong service court (i.e., into the one not diagonally opposite to the server), or falls short of the short service line or beyond the long service line, or outside the side boundary lines of the service court into which service is in order.

(c) If the server's feet are not in the service court from which service is at the time being in order, or if the feet of the player receiving the service are not in the service court diagonally opposite until the service is delivered. (Vide Law 16.)

(d) If, once the service has started, any player makes preliminary feints or otherwise intentionally baulks an opponent, or if any player deliberately delays serving the shuttle or delays getting ready to receive it so as to obtain an unfair advantage. (When the server and receiver have taken up their respective positions to serve and to receive, the first forward movement of this server's racket constitutes the start of the serve and such must be continuous thereafter.)

(e) If, either in service or play, the shuttle falls outside the boundaries of the court, or passes through or under the net, or fails to pass the net, or touches the roof or side walls, or the person or dress of a player. (A shuttle falling on a line shall be deemed to have fallen in the court or service court of which such line is a boundary.)

(f) If, when in play, the initial point of contact with the shuttle is not on the striker's side of the net. (The strike may, however, follow the shuttle over the net in the course of the stroke.)

(g) If, when the shuttle is "in play," a player touches the net or its supports with racket, person, or dress.

(h) If the shuttle be caught and held on the racket and then slung during the execution of a stroke; or if the shuttle be hit twice in succession by the same player with two strokes; or if the shuttle be hit by a player and his or her partner successively.

(i) If, in play, a player strikes the shuttle (unless he or she thereby makes a good return) or is struck by it, whether he or she is standing within or outside the boundaries of the court.

(j) If a player obstructs an opponent.

(k) If Law 16 be transgressed.

General

Rule 15

The server shall not serve till his opponent is ready, but the opponent shall be deemed to be ready if a return of the service be attempted.

Rule 16

The server and the player served to must stand within the limits of their respective service courts (as bounded by the short and long service, the center, and side lines), and some part of both feet of these players must remain in contact with the surface of the court in a stationary position until the service is delivered. A foot on or touching a line in the case of either the server or the receiver shall be held to be outside his or her service court (vide Law 14 (c)). The respective partners may take up any position, provided they do not unsight or otherwise obstruct an opponent.

Rule 17

(a) If, in the course of service or rally, the shuttle touches and passes over the net, the stroke is not invalidated thereby. It is a good return if the shuttle having passed outside either post drops on or within the boundary lines of the opposite court. A "Let" may be given by the umpire for any unforeseen or accidental hindrance.

(b) If, in service, or during a rally, a shuttle, *after passing over the net*, is caught in or on the net, it is a "Let."

(c) If the receiver is faulted for moving before the service is delivered, or for not being within the correct service court, in accordance with Laws 14(c) or 16, and at the same time the server is also faulted for a service infringement, it shall be a "Let."

(d) When a "Let" occurs, the play since the last service shall not count, and the player who served shall serve again except when Law 12 is applicable.

Rule 18

If the server, in attempting to serve, misses the shuttle, it is not a fault; but if the shuttle be touched by the racket, a service is thereby delivered.

Rule 19

If, when in play, the shuttle strikes the net and remains suspended there, or strikes the net and falls toward the surface of the court on the striker's side of the net, or hits the surface outside the court and an opponent then touches the net or shuttle with his racket or person, there is no penalty, as the shuttle is not *then* in play.

Rule 20

If a player has a chance of striking the shuttle in a downward direction when quite near the net, the opponent must not put up the racket near the net on the chance of the shuttle rebounding from it. This is obstruction within the meaning of Law 14(j).

Players may, however, hold up their rackets to protect their faces from being hit if they do not thereby baulk their opponent.

Rule 21

It shall be the duty of the umpire to call "fault" or "Let" should either occur, without appeal being made by the players, and to give a decision on any appeal regarding a point in dispute, if made before the next service; and also to appoint linespeople and service judges at his or her discretion. The umpire's decision shall be final, but he or she shall uphold the decision of a linesperson or service judge. This shall not preclude the umpire also from faulting the server or receiver. Where, however, a referee is appointed, an appeal shall lie to him or her from the decision of an umpire on questions of law only.

Continuous Play

Rule 22

(a) Play shall be continuous from the first service until the match is concluded; except (i) in international competitive events there shall be allowed an interval not exceeding five minutes between the second and third games of a match; (ii) in countries where conditions render it desirable, there shall be allowed, subject to the previously published approval of the national organization concerned, an interval not exceeding five minutes between the second and third games of a match, either singles or doubles or both; (iii) when necessitated by circumstances not within the control of the players, the umpire may suspend play for such a period as he or she may consider necessary. If play be suspended, the existing score shall stand and play be resumed from that point.

(b) Under no circumstances shall play be suspended to enable players to recover their strength or wind, or to receive instruction or advice.

(c) Except that in the case of an interval provided for the above, without the umpire's consent, no player shall be allowed to receive advice during a match or to leave the court until the match be concluded.

(d) The umpire shall be the sole judge of any suspension of play and he or she shall have the right to disqualify an offender.

NOTE

Intervals in Play as Sanctioned by the IBF

The international competitive events referred to in (a) (i) above are:

(1) The International Badminton Championship (Thomas Cup),

(2) The Ladies' International Badminton Championship (Uber Cup),

(3) The World Championships,

(4) All official international matches,

(5) National Open Championships and international championships of a higher status as sanctioned by the IBF.

Interpretations

1. Any movement or conduct by the server that has the effect of breaking the continuity of service after the server and receiver have taken their position to serve and to receive the service is a preliminary feint. For example, a server who, after having taken up a position to serve, delays hitting the shuttle for so long as to be unfair to the receiver, is guilty of such conduct. (Vide Law 14 (d).)

2. It is obstruction if a player invades an opponent's court with racket or person in any degree except as permitted in Law 14(f). (Vide Law 14 (j).)

3. Where necessary on account of the structure of a building, the local Badminton Authority may, subject to the right of veto of its National Organization, make bylaws dealing with cases in which a shuttle touches an obstruction.

Specification for Courts in International Play

The courts selected shall provide a minimum of 30 feet or 9 metres from floor to ceiling and there shall be at least 6 feet or 2 metres clear space surrounding all the outer lines of the courts, this space being also a minimum requirement between any two courts marked out side by side. This height shall be entirely free of girders and other obstructions over the area of the court. However, at all venues which are selected by the IBF, the measurements shall be subject to the approval of the Committee of Management for the competition concerned.

URT TSHIRT CO
CKS RACKET SO
D SHORTS C BI
HIRT COURT T
CKET SOCKS RA
TS C BIRD SHO
T TSHIRT COU
S RACKET SOC
SHORTS C BIRD
COURT TSHIRT
SOCKS RACKET
BIRD SHORTS C
URT TSHIRT CO

EQUIPMENT AND COURT

I t is important to get good equipment in badminton, just as it is in other sports. Buy the best you can afford; it will benefit your play.

RACKETS

Racket prices vary greatly. A tournament player will pay anywhere from $25 to $60 for a racket depending upon weight, strength, type of material, and appearance. The three major racket companies in the world today are Black Knight, Yonex, and Carlton. Black Knight and Yonex offer both wood frame and metal frame rackets while Carlton makes only metal frames. All three of these companies offer several different models utilizing different materials and at a variety of prices. As the author currently plays with Black Knight products, the rackets shown in Figure 4.1 are various types of Black Knight frames and shuttles. This does not signify that other rackets such as Yonex and Carlton are inferior. On the contrary, both are excellent rackets and in years past I have been sponsored by and used both brands with full satisfaction.

Figure 4.1

All wood frame rackets have either steel, aluminum, or graphite shafts. Metal frame rackets have steel, aluminum, or graphite frames and similar shafts as the wood rackets. The advantages of using metal frame rackets are (1) strength and (2) weight. The strength of the frame allows you to string very tight without danger of warping the head and the weight allows you to swing it quicker due to its lightness. Many metal rackets weigh between 90–120 grams which is quite light. There is some controversy among players and coaches as to the point at which "lightness" becomes an inhibitor of a powerful swing. A physicist would refer to the racket as the *mass. Force* = mass × *speed*. When the mass becomes too light, and speed cannot be increased to compensate for this factor, you cannot exert maximum force on the shuttle. It is highly probable that players with various sizes and strengths need different weight rackets to achieve maximum force. More research is needed before this question can satisfactorily be resolved.

Most rackets present from two to four grip sizes with the majority of players preferring either a small (3½") or a medium (3⅝") grip. Preference usually depends on the size of your hand and how comfortable the grip feels. Research seems to indicate that most players use too small a grip to achieve maximum power. Some players use the leather grip that comes on the racket but some replace this grip with a terry cloth "toweling" grip because they feel this can keep their hand dry from perspiration. Normally, tournament rackets are about 26" long and vary in weight from 3½ to 5 ounces. Most players who use the wood frame use gut because of its resiliency and "playability." These rackets, if strung tightly, must be kept in a press in order to prevent warping. Those who use the metal frame rackets string them with either gut or nylon. Presses are not needed as the frames do not warp. Gut is expensive and costs between $15–20. It is also difficult right now to find good quality gut. Gut is made from sheep and the best grades go to medical outlets for surgical use and the second grades are used for tennis and badminton rackets. Most of us who use metal frames find that a good grade of nylon holds up and plays just as well as gut. It also has the advantage of costing only $5–10.

SHUTTLECOCKS

The shuttlecock, or *shuttle*, as it will be called in this book, is manufactured in two different ways. The most expensive, but also the best for tournament play, is the feather shuttle. It is made of goose feathers, weighs from 73 to 85 grains, and has 14 to 16 feathers. The average shuttle used in the United States for most heated courts is a 76 grain, but the room temperature will determine the grain of shuttle used. All major tournaments and international matches try to have three or more different grains of shuttles on hand in case there is a wide variance in temperature. I have played in matches where the number of spectators caused the temperature in a building to increase enough that a lighter grain of shuttle was required. How can you tell if a shuttle is the proper weight? The rule book states that "a shuttle shall be deemed to be of correct pace if, when a player of average strength strikes it with a full underhand stroke from a spot immediately above one back boundary line, and at an upward angle, the shuttle falls not less than 1' and not more than 2'6" short of the other back boundary line.'' Controversy always surrounds the words "player of average strength" when evaluating if a shuttle is of the proper weight. Most tournament players know approximately where the shuttle should land for their own personal strength and ability when testing a shuttle. The author tests a shuttle and knows it is of proper weight when it lands at or 1' short of the deep doubles service line on the opposite side of the court when hit from behind the back boundary line. Mike Walker, who has won two national championships in men's doubles with the author, tests the shuttle by seeing if it lands at approximately the opposite back boundary line. This is a difference of 2'6" in our test but we both know it's the proper speed shuttle. Mike simply hits it harder and farther than I do in testing.

Feather shuttles cost from $1.20 to $1.40 each and last up to a maximum of one to two games with one-half of a game being about average. Most shuttles come in a tube of twelve. It is imperative that you treat your shuttles with utmost care to make them last longer. Some ways to increase the life of a shuttle are: (1) Run steam through the tube and cap it. This keeps the feathers moist for hours; (2) Run water over the feathers and also on the inside of the tube to keep feathers moist; (3) Wrap a wet towel around the tube to help keep feathers moist; and (4) devise a humidifier with either a wet sponge or a pan of water from which the shuttles can draw moisture. The best feather shuttles are made by Black Knight, Sportcraft, Yonex, H. L. International, and Rackets International.

Nylon shuttles cost from .50 to $1.00 and last up to several weeks. All high schools and colleges use nylon shuttles for activity classes and some high school leagues use the nylon shuttles for interscholastic competition. Recently, a few high school tournaments have used nylon shuttles and a few minor tournaments in England and Scotland have used nylon shuttles. It is fairly obvious that nylon shuttles save money. Unfortunately, those of us who play in tournaments have difficulty controlling the nylon shuttle and our "cut" shots (used for deception and control) are difficult if not impossible to use with nylon shuttles. Many companies are hard at work trying to design a nylon shuttle that will simulate the "playability" of the feather shuttle. If successful, it will be a blessing to those of us who regularly spend $5–10 per night for feather shuttles.

COURT

The official badminton court is illustrated in Figures 4.2A and 4.2B, showing a doubles and singles court. The net is stretched taut so that it is 5'1" at the net poles and 5' in the center of the court. If possible, the net poles should be placed on the side boundary lines of the doubles court. When this is not possible, the doubles sideline should be indicated by use of a thin post or strip of material. This post or material should be 1½" in width, fixed to the side boudary line and rise vertically to the net cord. Where this is in use on a court marked for doubles it shall be placed in the doubles sideline regardless of whether singles or doubles is being played. Lines should be 1½" wide to be legal and painted or taped on the floor.

Although you can play the game outdoors, all tournament and serious badminton must be played indoors where the shuttle is not affected by the elements. Occasionally tournaments are played on courts with ceilings less than 25' but this limits the types of shots you can hit. Most courts for national and international play are 30' or over in height.

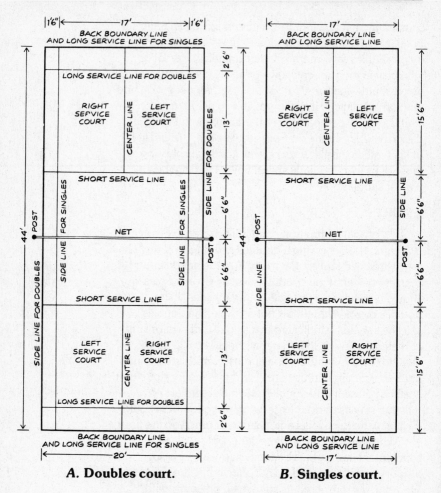

A. Doubles court.

B. Singles court.

Figure 4.2 *The badminton court.*

Most playing surfaces are regular hardwood floors, as you would suspect, since high school and college gymnasiums are the "homes" of badminton players. Recently the Southern California Badminton Association and the United States Badminton Association each acquired portable rubberized courts that can be laid over a hardwood floor. These courts are blue and have white lines on the surface. Most players like them because they eliminate all the other lines usually found on a gymnasium floor (basketball, volleyball, etc.).

Lighting can be a problem, especially in most high school, college, and YMCA gymnasiums where there are usually lights which can blind players momentarily as they look up to hit the shuttle. Most private badminton clubs in the United States and Canada place the lights between the courts rather than over the courts. The author has played in several of these clubs and the conditions are excellent. Most clubs paint the walls a dark color which further enhances the "playability" of the courts.

PLAYING APPAREL

Most badminton players wear casual clothes of any color for practices and tournaments. Items such as cotton T-shirts, shorts, tennis shoes, casual socks, and a warm-up suit or sweater are normal attire for men. Some men also wear shirts with collars for special occasions. Many women wear knit or cotton shirts or blouses and shorts while some still prefer tennis skirts or dresses.

There are still some clubs in Canada and other parts of the world where only white clothes can be worn on the courts. A few even expect that white warm-ups or sweaters should also be worn along with white clothes.

There are many excellent types of shoes on the market but be sure and buy a good pair with a good arch support and good tread which grips the court surface. Some players prefer a canvas top because of its lightness while others like the leather (or simulated leather) top because it seems to give better support and be more comfortable.

BASIC SKILLS

This is the most important chapter in the book for you must *first* learn basic skills as they act like the broad base of a pyramid which may be built on later as more advanced techniques and skills are added to the top. Each beginner must spend literally hours developing the proper stroking and footwork necessary to become a good player. Any drills used should, whenever possible, approximate a gamelike situation.

Material in this chapter will be presented in the following sequence:

1. Grips
2. Services
3. Overhead forehand strokes
4. Overhead backhand strokes
5. Underhand strokes
6. Analysis of performance

This order of presentation is my own personal preference and obviously you could learn them in any order. I favor this sequence for the following reasons:
(1) Grips are taught first because a "poor" grip can cause an inability to properly rotate the wrist and forearm.

(2) Services are taught next because of the unusual method of service that is required for playing badminton. As a legal serve must be hit upward with an underarm swing, learning it early allows you to practice it every time you start a rally especially while working on other basic strokes. (3) Overhead forehand strokes are taught next because the forehand is a more natural stroke than the backhand. Overhead forehands are also the predominant strokes in the game. (4) Overhead backhand strokes are taught next as a logical sequence after overhead forehands. (5) Underarm strokes are taught last. (Some instructors teach the underhand strokes after the service as they feel it is essentially the same type of upward stroke.) (6) An analysis of performance section has been placed at the end of the chapter to present most of the common faults in grips, services, and stroke production and some possible methods of correction.

GRIPS

There are three grips used in playing badminton: (1) forehand; (2) backhand; and (3) frying pan. The forehand grip may be used to the exclusion of the others, as some players find they can execute all the strokes

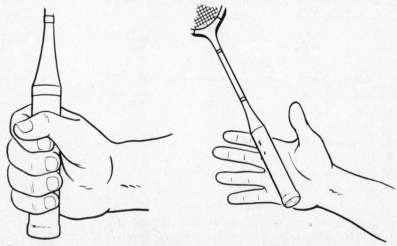

Figure 5.1A *Don't bunch fingers.*   **Figure 5.1B** *Racket should lay across palm and fingers.*

without changing their grip. Most players, however, do change their thumb slightly on the backhand. Each of the three grips will be explained below, but first there are a few points basic to all: (1) Hold the racket firmly but not too tightly; (2) Don't hold the racket with the fingers bunched together (see Figure 5.1A); and (3) Lay the racket across the palms and fingers so that it becomes an extension of your arm (see Figure 5.1B).

Forehand

Hold the racket by the throat in your left hand with the racket face at right angles to the floor. Place your right hand on the strings and slide it down the shaft and handle until the center of the heel of the hand rests on the butt end of the handle. Racket should be placed across the palm and fingers of the right hand as mentioned earlier. Looking down the racket with it at right angles to the floor, the "V" between your forehand and thumb should lie directly on the top of the grip. The forefinger should be separated a little from the others and look like a trigger finger on a pistol. The thumb will wrap naturally around the left side of the handle and all the fingers are spread slightly. This grip is called the *pistol grip* and closely resembles a handshake. (See Figure 5.2A)

Figure 5.2A

Summary of Forehand Grip

1. Lay racket across palm and fingers.
2. Separate forefinger from others to resemble a trigger finger on a pistol.
3. Wrap thumb around handle next to index finger.
4. Spread fingers.
5. "V" between forefinger and thumb points directly down top of grip.

Backhand

The only difference in the backhand grip from the forehand is that the thumb is moved from the wrapped-around side position to a more straightened position on the upper left-hand corner of the handle. This allows you to use the *inside* part of the thumb as leverage when rotating the hand and forearm on a backhand stroke. (See Figure 5.2B) Some teachers and coaches advocate the *flat-thumb* grip for backhand shots with the racket turned one-fourth of a turn to the right and the thumb placed flat on the handle. (See Figure 5.2C.) By pushing with the thumb as they hit the backhand, some players get a little more power than with the first method which emphasizes rotation of forearm and wrist. The author does not advocate this grip for advanced players, however, because a backhand shot cannot be hit effectively when the shuttle gets behind the body toward the back baseline.

Summary of Backhand (Inside of Thumb) Grip

1. Lay racket across palm and fingers.
2. Separate forefinger and other fingers as with the forehand grip.
3. Straighten thumb and place it along top side level of the handle.
4. Use inside of thumb to rotate wrist and forearm on backhand stroke.
5. "V" between forefinger and thumb is same as forehand grip.

Figure 5.2B

Figure 5.2C

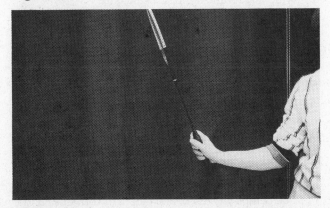

Figure 5.2D

Summary of Backhand (Flat Thumb) Grip

1. Lay racket across palm and fingers.
2. Rotate racket one-fourth turn to right.
3. Forefinger and other fingers are similar to forehand grip.
4. Place flat part of thumb on back of grip in a straightened position.
5. Gain power by pushing with thumb.
6. "V" between forefinger and thumb points down left side of grip.

Frying Pan

This grip is used primarily in doubles play for service, service returns, and net play where only a short stroke is needed. Some players feel it gives them more control and quickness on these short strokes. *Do not* use this grip for singles play or doubles play from deep in the court. As the grip is shortened, you can only play a forehand stroke with this grip and it is also difficult to get power. Lay the racket on the floor and pick it up with the racket face parallel to your body. Racket should feel like you are swinging a frying pan or hammer. Butt of the racket will extend an inch or two below the palm (see Figure 5.2D).

Summary of Frying Pan Grip

1. Hold racket at junction of grip and shaft with butt end extending below palm one or two inches.
2. Wrap fingers and thumb around grip.
3. "V" between forefinger and thumb is on left side of grip.
4. Hold racket head up in a perpendicular position, with palm facing net, on all overhead shots.

SERVICES

There are three criteria that must be satisfied for a legal service. These are: (1) Server must stand within limits of the service court and must have some part of both feet in contact with floor until service is delivered; (2) At moment of being struck, the shuttle must not be higher than the server's waist; and (3) The head of the racket must be completely below any part of the server's hand holding the racket at the moment the shuttle is struck.

Both the server and the receiver must remain stationary but not so their respective partners. Partners may move or take any position on the court, provided they do not *unsight* the receiver as shuttle is struck on the serve. (This would be illegal and result in loss of service.) In top national and international matches and tournaments, there are umpires and service judges who watch for these three service criteria. Service judges call faults on the servers and umpires call faults on the receivers.

High Deep Service

Developing a high deep serve is very important, particularly in singles, as it immediately sends your opponent to the baseline of the court and forces that player to make a good shot to regain the attack. A weak return allows you to take the offensive. To execute this service, take a position approximately 3–4 feet in back of the short service line, with the left foot forward. Stand comfortably with your feet spread between 12″ and 18″ apart and your weight mostly on the right foot. In the starting position, your left shoulder should point toward the receiver. Your right arm is extended away from the body and the racket is held behind you about waist high with wrist flexed radially (to thumb side). Your left arm is extended away from the body and held high between your head and chest (with the shuttle gripped at the base between thumb and forefinger. (See Figure 5.3A.)

As you drop the shuttle (do not toss it) with your left hand well ahead of your body, the racket is swung down and forward. Shift your weight from back to front foot as you rotate your body to the left, so that at contact point, it faces the direction of the shuttle's flight (see Figure 5.3B). Rotate your wrist to a straightened position at contact point with the shuttle, which should be well ahead of your body and between knee and waist level. Notice also that your right arm is straightened at point of contact (see Figure 5.3C). Immediately after contact there is a rapid inward rotation (called *pronation*) of wrist and forearm as the racket is swung upward. *Important point*: Wrist is *rotated* and not snapped as some books indicate! (See Figure 5.3D.) Follow through of the racket is high and over your left shoulder as wrist and forearm continue to rotate (see Figure 5.3E and 5.3F). The entire racket path is like an up and down pendulum swing.

After the shuttle has left the racket, step across and straddle the center service line. This is the *base* to which you should attempt to return after each shot of a rally. Figure 5.9 shows the trajectory of a good high deep serve. The shuttle should be served high enough to clear your opponent's racket and if not hit by the opponent, should land in the last two feet of the singles court near the baseline. Height of shuttle will vary from 10 to 25 feet above ground when hit to the opponent's court depending on your preference.

Summary of Deep Singles Service

1. Stand 3–4 feet in back of short singles service line.
2. Spread feet between 12–18″ apart with weight on back foot.

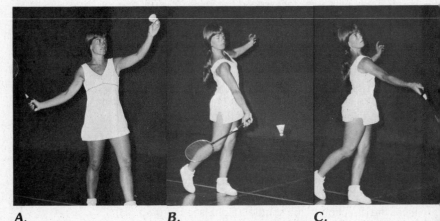

A.   B.   C.

Figures 5.3A–5.3F *High deep service.*

3. Extend both arms away from body and flex wrist radially (to thumb side).
4. As you drop shuttle well ahead of body, shift weight to front foot and start to rotate wrist.
5. Hit shuttle ahead of body between knee and hip high with straightened wrist.
6. After you strike the shuttle rapidly rotate wrist and forearm inward (pronation of wrist and forearm).
7. Follow through is high and across left shoulder.
8. Hit shuttle between 10–25 feet high (your preference) to land in the last two feet of service court.
9. Do not move either foot until shuttle has left the racket.
10. Do not push the shuttle — hit it!

E.   F.

Low Short Service (Forehand)

This serve is used more in doubles than in singles but can be effective in singles if used at the right time. If serving low in singles, do so from the same position as stated earlier for the high deep service — 3–4 feet back of short service line. If serving low in doubles, most players stand about 1–2 feet from the short service line. This is done for two reasons: (1) server can cover all net shots quicker if standing closer to short service line; and (2) standing closer gives opponent less time to see the shuttle as that person attempts to make a service return.

Many players unknowingly violate the rule on service that deals the "racket head above any part of hand." Be sure and keep the shaft of the racket at a 45 degree angle downward so that no part of the hand (including fingers) is touching any part of a line that is parallel to the floor and parallel to the lowest part of the head of the racket. Figure 3.2 from Chapter 3 shows the correct and incorrect ways to hold the racket head at point of contact.

To execute the forehand low service, take a stance very similar to the one on the high serve with the left foot and left side of the body nearest the net. Because little power is needed on this low serve, the arm position is quite different than in the high deep serve. Bring both arms closer to the body with the racket and shuttle held considerably lower than in previous service (see Figure 5.4). By holding it closer and lower, there is not a great time lapse between dropping the shuttle and hitting it. This gives your opponent less time to see and rush your serve. Most players shift their weight to the front foot *before* the stroke is started.

The shuttle should be contacted close to waist level and slightly more to the player's right than in the high deep serve. The racket comes around the body unlike the up and down pendulum swing on the deep serve. Be careful you don't violate the "racket head above hand" rule, though, as the racket swings around the body. Guide the shuttle over the net with a gentle sweeping motion made with the wrist in a cocked position. There are two reasons for not uncocking the wrist: (1) If you hit with the wrist, you lose control and the shuttle might pop

Figure 5.4 *Starting position of the low short serve (forehand).*

up over the net where your opponent could kill it (also, the shuttle travels only a short distance and does not need the power of a wrist snap); and (2) keeping the wrist cocked gives you the threat of a *flick* serve, a change of pace serve where a quick motion of the wrist allows you to hit a serve over an opponent's racket into the deep portion of the service court.

The shuttle should reach its maximum height just before reaching the net tape and commence to fall as it goes over the net. Shuttle should cross net within 1–2 inches of the net tape. A good serve will land within the first six inches past the short service line. Very little body rotation is needed and the stroke is quite short. Figure 5.9 shows the trajectory of a good low serve.

Summary of Low Short Service (Forehand)

1. Stand 1–2 feet in back of short service line.
2. Spread feet 10–15 inches apart with weight on front foot.
3. Hold arms close to the body.
4. Contact shuttle ahead of and to the right of body with wrist cocked.
5. Sweep shuttle across the net — do not hit it!
6. Keep wrist firm and in radially flexed position during the entire swing.
7. Shuttle should cross net within 1–2 inches of net tape and land within first 6 inches past short service line.
8. Do not move either foot until shuttle has left the racket.

Low Short Service (Backhand)

This method of serving started in the Far East in the last 1950s and early 1960s by the Indonesians. It spread rapidly to Malaysia and then to Europe and America. In the past ten years it has been adopted by about 50 percent of the U. S. tournament players at all levels. Why is it so popular? Probably because of the many advantages it has over the forehand serve. These are: (1) the shuttle is harder to see as it is hidden against your clothes (especially if your wear white); (2) because it is hit in front of you, the shuttle takes less time to cross the net;

Figure 5.5 *Starting position of the low short serve (backhand).*

(3) the shuttle is harder to see because of the shortened swing necessary to hit it; and (4) the added threat of a flick serve which is very difficult to see as it goes over your head. All of these combine to force most service receivers to abandon an all-out aggressive rush and start to play finesse shots to various spots on the court. This gives the serving team more time to hit their next shot with a reasonable chance of success.

To execute the backhand low service, most players stand just past the short service line. As previously described with the forehand low service, this gives the opponent less time to see the shuttle as it crosses the net and it also allows you to cover the net returns much quicker. The starting stance should be with both feet square to the net and about 1–2 feet apart. Some players like to drop the right foot back a little off the line as they feel more comfortable in that stance. Hold the racket in a shortened backhand grip with the thumb in a straightened flat position on the back of the grip. Hold the shuttle in front of you by the feathers (or nylon skirt) and anchor the left elbow to the left side of the body to establish a consistent hitting location. Hold the right arm away from the body with the upper arm extended and the elbow almost shoulder high. Extend the forearm downward and position the racket head and shaft at a 45 degree angle downward. Another change from the forehand serve is that many players look at their opponent and not the shuttle when executing this service (see Figure 5.5). Make the stroke itself without moving the shoulder or upper arm. Move the forearm and hand forward as you drop the shuttle and stroke the shuttle gently o er the net. The stroke is a sweep of the forearm and hand and not a hard hit which might pop the shuttle up over the net where the service receiver might smash it to the floor. The shuttle should cross the net within 1–2 inches of the net and land on the first 6 inches just past the short service line. See Figure 5.9 for proper trajectory of the low serve.

Summary of Low Short Service (Backhand)

1. Stand close to short service line with feet square to line.
2. Use a shortened backhand grip with thumb in a straightened position on back of grip.
3. Hold shuttle by feathers or nylon skirt.
4. Anchor left elbow to left side of body.
5. Hold right arm away from body with elbow almost shoulder high.
6. Position racket head and shaft at a 45 degree angle downward.
7. Stroke shuttle gently with forearm and hand.
8. Shuttle should cross within 1–2 inches of net and land within first 6 inches past short service line.
9. Do not move either foot until shuttle has left racket.

OVERHEAD FOREHAND STROKES

General Mechanics of All Overhead Forehand Strokes

The author is indebted to two friends from Canada for much of the material contained in the following sections on the general mechanics of both overhead forehand and overhead backhand strokes. Although I have analyzed badminton players and their swings for many years, I have not used very high speed photography to verify my beliefs. Barbara A. Gowitzke and David B. Waddell of Hamilton, Ontario have filmed at 200 and 400 frames per second and analyzed these strokes and written several papers since 1977 on the results of their research. I have found that their papers are excellent and wholeheartedly endorse their findings.

These same mechanics discussed below are used for all three overhead strokes of clear, drop, and smash. Strive to make all three strokes look the same. This will make your strokes deceptive, so your opponent cannot tell which stroke you are playing until the shuttle is actually hit. The only differences among these three strokes are: (1) the contact point of racket; (2) the power imparted to shuttle; and (3) the direction in which the shuttle leaves the racket.

The overhead forehand strokes as illustrated in Figures 5.6A–E are usually made from the back half and in the middle or on the forehand (right) side of the court. While waiting for the shuttle to be struck by your opponent, stand in the *ready position*, which is with feet and shoulders parallel to the net, racket held with grip at waist level, and racket head around shoulder level, held slightly on the backhand side, and with knees bent (see Figure 6.1). This position is about 4–5 feet behind the intersection of the short service line and the center service line (commonly known as the "T"). As the shuttle is hit up to your forehand side, turn your body so that your feet are perpendicular to the net and your left shoulder is pointed toward the net. Start to skip sideways (or back pedal if necessary) until you are slightly behind the flight of the dropping shuttle (see Chapter 6 for footwork). This will be your *hitting stance*.

Hold the racket in front of your body until the entire swing starts. From this "ready position," with the wrist flexed to the thumb side and the racket head at right angles to the hitting direction, the actual swing is begun (see Figure 5.6A). Draw the racket back quickly, with the racket head sweeping across your head and down your back and across to a position directly behind your right shoulder (see Figure 5.6B). Follow by deeply flexing the elbow with the right hand behind the head. As this is happening, the lower portion of the body has also started to come into play. As you flex your elbow, start to rotate the trunk and hips with your weight shifted to the left leg (see Figure 5.6C). Follow by a rapid extension of the elbow both forward and upward from behind your back. Just before contact point, rotate the upper arm, forearm, and wrist inward (pronate) which brings the racket face to a position perpendicular to the direction of the shuttle (see

Figure 5.6A   **Figure 5.6B**   **Figure 5.6C**

Figure 5.6D). Your elbow is now almost fully extended and this pronation of forearm causes rapid acceleration of the racket head which imparts speed and power to the shuttle. By contact point, the weight is completely on the left leg. A moment after contact, continue to rotate the upper arm, forearm, and wrist very rapidly so that the elbow finishes high and slightly flexed, the racket head finishes down, and the hitting surface of the racket faces the observer standing to the right side of player hitting the stroke (see Figure 5.6E). Complete follow through finds the racket drifting across to the left side of the body.

It is important to start this entire swing with the racket held in front of the body at the *ready position*. By starting the backswing and continuing to the forward swing without pausing, the muscles of the racket arm are put "on stretch" during the backswing which imparts additional power to the stroke on the forward swing.

Figure 5.6D   **Figure 5.6E**

Summary of Overhead Forehand Mechanics

1. Flex wrist to thumb side and start entire swing from position with racket in front of body.
2. Draw racket back quickly, with racket head sweeping down the back to a position behind the right shoulder.
3. Flex elbow deeply and suspend wrist behind head.
4. Rotate trunk and hips to face net at contact point of racket.
5. Rapidly extend elbow both forward and upward from behind your head.
6. Rotate upper arm, forearm, and wrist inward (pronate) to bring racket face to a position perpendicular to direction of the hit.
7. Shortly after contact with shuttle, continue to pronate the forearm which causes the racket head to point toward the floor.
8. On the follow through, drift the racket and arm across to left side of body.

Forehand Clear

This stroke is meant to hit the shuttle high and deep into the opposing court as close to the back boundary as possible. (See Figure 5.9 for proper trajectory of an overhead clear.) The racket face must be tilted *upward* at contact point, because the shuttle must go upward at least high enough to clear your opponent's extended racket, forcing that player to the back portion of the court in order to make a return. The height of the clear will vary between 9 and 20 feet as it crosses the middle of your opponent's court. The amount of power needed will vary but it is usually hit hard with rapid inward rotation of upper arm, forearm, and wrist (pronation). It is also important to contact the shuttle ahead of your body whenever possible, otherwise you are going to be falling backward and be out of position for your next shot.

Key Points for the Forehand Clear:

1. Hit shuttle with racket face tilted up for upward trajectory.
2. Contact shuttle in front of body.

3. Rotate forearm and wrist to bring racket face flat to target area at contact point.

4. Hit shuttle *hard*.

Forehand Drop

This stroke is meant to hit the shuttle so that it will barely go over the net and land as close to the net as possible. (See Figure 5.9 for proper trajectory of an overhead drop shot.) It is a slow shot that is hit with a soft pushing motion with the racket face perpendicular to the floor or pointed slightly downward at point of contact. Be sure to follow through on this shot or you will lose accuracy. A good way to practice this shot is to try to hit the shuttle with *no* sound at point of contact. This will ensure that you impact it softly. You cannot hit it with absolutely no sound, but the attempt helps you keep from hitting it to the middle of your opponent's court. The drop is usually directed to the front corners of the net to make your opponent move out of the center of the court in order to hit a return. Be careful you don't overuse this stroke as it is slower than the other types of shots and gives your opponent more time to react to it. Also, if the shuttle is continually going too deep into your opponent's court, hit the shuttle *slightly* upward so it loops.

Key Points for the Forehand Drop:

1. Hit shuttle with a flat or slightly downward trajectory.

2. Stroke shuttle gently over the net — do *not* hit it *hard*!

3. Try to hit your drop shot with no sound at point of contact.

4. Follow through on the stroke for accuracy and control. Do not stop as shuttle is contacted.

5. Loop the shuttle if your shots are continually landing too deep in opponent's court.

Forehand Smash

This stroke is meant to hit the shuttle down as hard as possible but with accuracy into the opposing court. (See Figure 5.9 for proper trajectory of an overhead smash.) The racket face must be tilted downward at contact point with as much angle as possible. Remember that the smash is the *point winner*. Clears and drops move your opponent around and eventually force him or her to hit a weak return that you must put away with your smash. The smash is the *finisher* of the rally and wins points for you. It is normally not used in the back 2½ feet of the court (except in doubles) because it decelerates rapidly after it has traveled a great distance. Angle is more important than the speed of your smash, so contact the shuttle from as high a position as possible with arm extended. Contact shuttle ahead of your body and rotate the forearm and wrist rapidly (pronate) and very forcibly so that the shuttle travels downward at a rapid speed. The smash is usually directed within 1–2 feet of the sidelines, but an occasional smash at your opponent's body is also quite effective.

Key Points for the Forehand Smash:

1. Do not smash from deeper than three-fourths from the back of the court, as the shuttle slows down very rapidly.
2. Contact the shuttle ahead of body with arm extended.
3. At contact point, have racket pointing downward.
4. Rotate forearm and wrist very rapidly as contact is made.
5. A sharp *downward* angle is usually more important than sheer speed.
6. Hit shuttle *hard*!

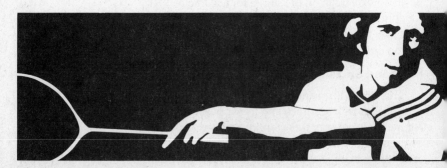

OVERHEAD BACKHAND STROKES

General Mechanics of the Overhead Backhand Strokes

As with the overhead forehand strokes, try to use the same windup and swing for the overhead backhands until the very last moment before contact. This makes your shots deceptive and hard to anticipate by your opponent.

The overhead backhand strokes, as illustrated in Figures 5.7A–F, are usually played from the back half and on the left side of the court. Stand in the *ready position* (explained earlier and in Figure 6.1) until your opponent hits the shuttle up to your backhand (left) side of the court. Start your move toward the backhand corner by taking a small step with your left foot and immediately starting to pivot on your left leg (see Figure 5.7A). This is followed by a crossover step with the right leg which now faces the left sideline — sometimes it even faces the back baseline and your back is to your opponent. Draw racket head back quickly and start to move downward as the elbow points up toward the shuttle (see Figure 5.7B). At this point in the stroke, your weight is shifting to the racket foot and your racket head is continuing to point downward toward the floor. Look at the shuttle over the right shoulder. With very little pause at the end of the backswing, start the forward swing by rapidly extending the elbow upward, pulling the butt end of the racket upward (see Figure 5.7C). Weight is now completely on the racket leg and foot as the upper arm, forearm, and wrist rotate outward (supinate) quickly (see Figure 5.7D). At contact point, the racket face is pointing slightly upward or perpendicular to the floor depending on stroke desired. The racket face is at right angles to the direction of the shot and the elbow and arm extended up and to side of the body. (See Figure 5.7E.) After the shuttle has left the racket, continue to rotate the forearm and wrist so that racket face now points toward the floor on the follow through. The elbow also seems to "back up" as contact is made with the shuttle as viewed from the side of the court (see Figure 5.7F). It is important to start the overhead backhand strokes by turning and dropping the racket head down toward the floor (or around the body). Either place is acceptable. This is immediately followed by the forward part of the swing upward toward the shuttle. This puts the muscles "on stretch" when you do not stop the swing with the racket head downward toward the floor and adds power to your forward stroke. One good method of practicing the backhand overhead is to stand near an 8–9 foot wall and swing upward with a towel. Hold the towel at one end and shift your weight to the racket foot and extend the towel upward with a rapid outward rotation of upper arm, forearm, and wrist, trying to snap the towel up on the wall. This action very closely simulates the actual movement of the racket during backhand overhead strokes.

Figure 5.7A   **Figure 5.7B**   **Figure 5.7C**

Summary of Overhead Backhand Mechanics

1. Step across with right leg to left sideline (or even toward baseline) and show your back to opponent.
2. Draw racket back quickly so that racket head points toward floor with elbow at shoulder height.
3. After reaching full backswing, immediately start to bring butt of racket upward by raising elbow and hand upward. This must be done with no pause at end of backswing.
4. Shift weight completely to racket leg while rotating upper arm, forearm, and wrist outward (supinate).
5. At contact point, extend elbow completely and hold the racket face pointing upward or perpendicular to floor depending on stroke desired.
6. Shortly after contact, the elbow appears to "back up" as you continue to rotate forearm and wrist until racket face points to floor on follow through.

Figure 5.7D   **Figure 5.7E**   **Figure 5.7F**

Backhand Clear

As in the forehand clear, the object is to hit the shuttle high and deep into the opposing court as close to the back boundary line as possible. (See Figure 5.9 for proper trajectory of overhead clear.) Tilt the racket face *upward* at contact point, so shuttle can clear your opponent's extended racket, forcing that player to go to the back portion of the court to make a return. Power will vary but it is usually hit as hard as possible with rapid outward rotations of upper arm, forearm, and wrist (supination). It is also important to contact the shuttle ahead of body whenever possible.

Key Points for the Backhand Clear:

1. Hit shuttle with racket face tilted upward.
2. Contact shuttle in front of body.
3. Upper arm, forearm, and wrist are rotated to bring racket face flat to target area at contact point.
4. Shuttle should be hit hard!

Backhand Drop

The idea is to hit the shuttle so that it will barely go over the net and land close to the net. (See Figure 5.9 for proper trajectory of overhead drop shot.) It is a slow shot that is hit with a soft pushing motion with the racket face perpendicular to the floor or pointed slightly downward at point of contact. Be sure to also follow through for better control and accuracy. The backhand drop is usually directly to front corners of the net to make an opponent move out of the center of the court to make the return.

Key Points for the Backhand Drop:

1. Hit shuttle with a flat or slightly downward trajectory.
2. Stroke shuttle gently over the net — do not hit it *hard*!
3. Try to hit drop shot with *no* sound.
4. Follow through for better control and accuracy.
5. Loop the shuttle slightly if your shots are continually landing too deep in opponent's court.

UNDERHAND STROKES

In general, the hitting stance for all underhand strokes (with the exception of the smash returns discussed later in Chapter 7) is to hit with the racket foot closest to the net. This applies on both forehand and backhand underhand strokes. By making your last step before shuttle contact with the racket foot, you are able to reach about one foot further than off the opposite foot and also this body position makes it easier to make cross-court returns on both drops and clears. The racket face should be parallel to the floor with wrist cocked and weight shifted to the racket foot just before shuttle contact. Shuttle should be contacted as soon as possible and as close to net height as practical (see Figure 5.8).

These underhand strokes are usually played somewhere between the short service line and the net. As they are the reply to a drop shot, they are often played below net height and sometimes even within a few inches of the floor.

Figure 5.8

Forehand Net Clear

This stroke is almost identical to the singles deep service with the exception that the racket foot is closest to the net. As you move to the net for this stroke, the racket shoulder should turn toward the net and the wrist should be cocked. Just before contact with the shuttle, shift your weight to the racket foot and rotate your forearm and wrist inward while lifting upward the forearm. (See Figure 5.9 for proper trajectory.) Try to keep the backswing short for added deception. The elbow will finish slightly flexed. Cross-court clears must be hit harder as they have a longer distance to travel before reaching the baseline. The shuttle should be hit at least high enough to clear an opponent's upstretched racket in the center of his or her court.

Backhand Net Clear

Keep racket shoulder and foot nearest the net and the wrist cocked slightly as you move into a hitting position. Use a backhand grip for this stroke. Shift your weight to racket foot just before contact and use a lifting of the arm and outward rotation of forearm and wrist to get the desired loft on the shuttle. Keep backswing short for added deception. Elbow again will finish slightly flexed and the shuttle is hit high and deep to the back of your opponent's court. As mentioned earlier on forehand net clear, hit the shuttle high enough to clear your opponent's outstretched racket and hit it harder on cross-court clears as it must travel a longer distance to the back baseline. (Straight ahead clears can only travel 22' while cross-court clears may travel 28' and still be in the court when they land.)

Key Points for the Underhand Net Clears:

1. Contact shuttle as close to the net height as possible.
2. Turn the right shoulder slightly toward the net.
3. Keep right foot always forward (both forehand and backhand).
4. Cock wrist as you move toward the net.
5. Rotate forearm and wrist to provide the power to hit the shuttle high and deep (inward for forehand and outward for backhand).

Forehand Net Drop

As mentioned earlier, the racket shoulder and foot should be nearest the net as the shuttle is hit. Keep wrist cocked and contact as near to the top of the net as possible. The shuttle should be gently hit just over the net trying to keep the shuttle as close to net height as possible to prevent an opponent from killing your return. Little or no wrist is used. It is a lifting motion of the entire arm and racket hand. This drop is sometimes called a "hairpin" because of its trajectory (see Figure 5.9).

Backhand Net Drop

This is the same as the forehand with racket foot closest to the net. The only major difference is that a backhand grip is used. Contact the shuttle as close to net height as possible. This gives your opponent less time to see and reach your return.

Key Points for the Net Drops:

1. Contact the shuttle as close to net height as possible.
2. Wrist is cocked (and remains cocked) as the shuttle is stroked gently over the net (with a lifting motion).
3. Loop the shuttle so it will land close to the net on the opposing side.
4. Do not pop the shuttle, *guide* it over the net.

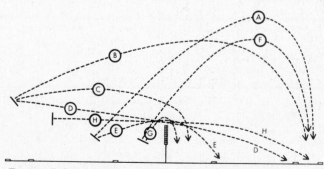

Figure 5.9 *Trajectory of the different strokes.*

A. Singles (Deep) Serve.
B. Clear.
C. Drop.
D. Smash.
E. Doubles (Low) Serve.
F. Net Clear.
G. Net (Hairpin) Drop.
H. Drives.

ANALYSIS OF THE BASIC SKILLS

Difficulty	Probable Cause	Suggested Correction
I. *Deep Serves* Missing shuttle entirely on deep serve.	1. Holding shuttle too long before dropping it. 2. Starting racket swing before dropping shuttle. 3. Unable to coordinate both arms at proper time.	1. Shuttle is dropped first *before* racket is started downward and drop is made in front of body toward the net. 2. Racket contact with shuttle should take place ahead of body and approximately at knee height so shuttle is dropped first and then swing starts. 3. Bring arms close to body and raise right hand and elbow upward. Shuttle is then hit out of left hand holding shuttle next to head of racket. Extend arms downward as success achieved at various levels so that eventually the full swing is accomplished.
Hitting shuttle upward on deep serve so it goes only half court.	1. Holding shuttle too long before dropping it. 2. Racket face pointing upward at contact with shuttle. 3. Swinging with arm only — sweeping shuttle. 4. Snapping wrist upward at contact.	1. Drop shuttle to knee height before contact is made with racket. 2. Racket face must be pointing at approximately a 45 degree angle from vertical at contact. Adjust angle if necessary to get desired depth in court of the shuttle. 3. Radially cock wrist and uncock it to a straight position at point of contact. Rotate arm and wrist (pronate) forcibly after contact and follow through over left shoulder. 4. Similar to #3. Wrist should be radially cocked (to thumb side) and uncocked at point of contact to a straightened position. Arm and wrist immediately rotate after contact to give power to the shuttle. Contact shuttle at 45 degree racket angle from vertical.

Difficulty	Probable Cause	Suggested Correction
II. *Low Serves* Hitting shuttle too high on low serve (or inconsistency in low serve).	1. Using too much wrist in the swing.	1. Wrist should be radially cocked and maintained in this position throughout entire swing because racket must *sweep* shuttle over net and not strike with uncocking of the wrist. This is the best way to develop a consistent serve that may be repeated with success.
III. *Forehand Overhead Swings* Inability to hit shuttle deep into opponent's court and/or hit it hard on a smash.	1. Facing net with shoulder square to net as you start to swing. 2. Stepping forward with racket foot as you start to swing. 3. Not pronating forearm and wrist on shuttle contact. 4. Starting forward swing from a position with the racket behind head and pointing down the back.	1. Point nonracket shoulder at net as you line up to swing. This means you must rotate hips and shoulders to get racket into a proper hitting position. This rotation adds power and deception to your swing. 2. This goes along with #1 in that you must step forward with nonracket foot, shift weight to this foot, and rotate hips and shoulders to get proper power to the swing. (Advanced players should ignore this section as they might hit the shuttle while off the ground. See "Switch Step" in Chapter 6.) 3. Forearm and wrist must move from radially cocked position as racket is swung upward to an uncocked straightened position at contact. This is followed immediately by a pronation of wrist and forearm (inward rotation) to get maximum power. 4. Entire swing must be made (from ready position to complete follow through) without stopping. This swing is as follows: (1) Racket starts in front of body, (2) racket swings behind head, (3) racket continues down the back as upper body rotates, (4) racket swings up to contact shuttle with extended elbow and arm over head, (5) arm and wrist pronate, (6) racket finishes pointed toward floor, and (7) drifts across to left side of body on follow through. This entire swing must take place without stopping to put the muscles used "on stretch" which provides maximum power to the swing.

ANALYSIS OF THE BASIC SKILLS (CONT.)

Difficulty	Probable Cause	Suggested Correction
Inability to hit overheads properly due to improper racket angle at contact.	1. Not having a basic understanding of way shuttle reacts off racket face and position racket face must be in to get the proper trajectory on your shots.	1. Shuttle always comes off racket face at 90 degree angle to position of racket. On clears, racket must point upward; on drops, racket must point forward (or slightly up or down); and on smashes, racket must point downward. The smash is a good example of a "poor basic understanding" by many students — racket swing must start *sooner* on a smash because racket face must move the most distance after the arm is extended to get into a downward hitting position (about 1 to 1½ feet further than for a clear).
Inability to hit overheads properly due to the shuttle getting too far *behind* player toward baseline.	1. Being lazy, slow of foot, or not hustling to get behind shuttle (towards baseline) whenever possible.	1. Emphasize *getting behind* shuttle on all shots. This cannot always be done but should be possible on a return of a deep serve. Back pedal quickly so you are actually standing outside the back baseline and then move *forward* to hit your service return. This gives added power to your stroke and also gives you the added advantage of forward movement which helps you return to the ready position in the center of the court to await your opponent's next shot. Obviously, you should do this on all overheads when possible.
Contact of shuttle with bent arm.	1. Not extending forearm, hand, and racket *upward* as stroke is made. 2. Letting shuttle drop too low and/or not raising elbow while swinging.	1. Emphasize upward motion of arm to contact shuttle with straight arm and as high as you can comfortably reach. One drill for this is to extend upward and hit the basketball net which extends down from the basketball goal. This is vitally important in hitting smashes for hitting with a straight arm allows you to get a better downward angle on your shot. 2. Similar to #1 — extend *upward* to hit shuttle with straight arm. Another drill is to suspend a shuttle on a string downward from the ceiling (or a ceiling beam, etc.) and practice hitting upward to meet shuttle with a straight arm.

Difficulty	Probable Cause	Suggested Correction
IV. *Backhand Overhead Swings* Inability to hit shuttle deep into opponent's court.	1. Facing net with shoulders square to net as you start to swing.	1. It is impossible to hit a good backhand overhead shot without turning and actually having your back facing the net at moment of contact with the shuttle. Your racket foot will be pointing toward your backhand corner also at this moment of contact.
	2. Not shifting weight to racket foot as you start to swing.	2. Weight is shifted to racket foot shortly before shuttle contact and entire body move over the racket foot as swing is made for maximum power.
	3. Not supinating forearm and wrist as shuttle is contacted.	3. Use the simple phrase "thumb down to thumb up" to describe the supinating movement of the forearm and wrist. An excellent drill for developing the backhand overhead strokes is to use a towel and slap it up on a wall. This closely resembles the swing of the forearm and wrist on the backhand overhead strokes. Stand about one foot from the wall when practicing and strive to hit the wall with the towel at a vertical position above the hand.
	4. Starting forehand swing from a position with the racket head pointing toward the floor.	4. Similar to the forehand overhead strokes listed earlier, the "probable cause" and "suggested correction" for No. 4 emphasizes taking a full backswing followed immediately by the forward swing. The same must be done on the backhand overhead strokes. The backhand swing is as follows: (1) racket starts in front of body, (2) racket swings around body as racket foot steps toward baseline, (3) racket head swings down to point at floor (thumb down), (4) racket is pulled up by butt end as hand extends upward, (5) racket head is extended upward by supinating forearm and wrist (thumb up), (6) after contact with shuttle, the hand rotates over so face of racket points downward.
	5. Contacting shuttle too close to body. (Overhead)	5. Contact with shuttle should be made out to the side of body. Most common error is extending arm upward too close to body which becomes very awkward looking and not as efficient as contacting to the side. Racket itself is vertical to ground at contact.

ANALYSIS OF THE BASIC SKILLS (CONT.)

Difficulty	Probable Cause	Suggested Correction
V. *Underhand Strokes* Letting shuttle get too low (below net level) before making contact with the shuttle and/or contact with wrong foot nearest the net.	1. Either laziness or a lack of understanding of the importance of making contact on underhand shots as near net height as possible.	1. Have a partner stand near the net and "toss" a shuttle over close to the net on either your forehand or backhand side. Starting from the ready position in the center of the court, take a couple of quick steps and make a *lunging* move toward the shuttle and contact it as high as possible. This lunge move is very similar to a fencing lunge and should *always* result in landing with the racket foot nearest the net (on both forehand and backhand). It is important to have the racket foot nearest the net on all underhand shots for two reasons: (1) you can reach about one foot farther from this position, and (2) it is easier to hit cross-court drops and clears than when feet are in opposite position. Start by hitting net shot returns to the "tosses" by your partner. After this becomes easy, add the underhand clears and eventually learn to hit either shot from this high position.

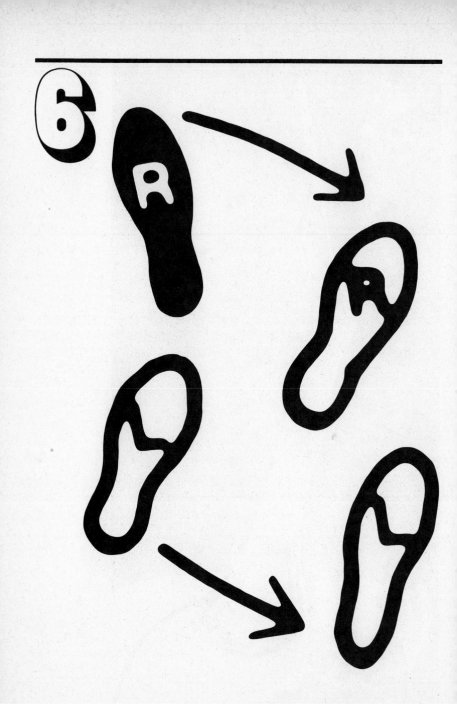

FOOTWORK

The object of good footwork is to move as efficiently as possible to all areas of the court. There are six basic spots to which you must be able to move effectively, play your shot, and return to the center of the court. Although you should try to get back to the center of the court after each shot, it is more important to *not* be moving as your opponent strikes the shuttle. If you cannot get completely back to the center of the court, stop wherever you are just before your opponent hits the shuttle.

Each of the six spots will be broken down individually. Footwork is very important, for you can neither hit the shuttle efficiently nor control your opponent if you cannot easily get into position to hit. An important point to remember in badminton is that the last step before the shuttle is struck should always be taken with the right foot (racket foot). This will be emphasized in the material on the six basic spots listed below.

READY POSITION

When assuming the ready position, keep the feet even and spread a little wider than the shoulders. The knees should be bent with the weight on the balls of the feet. The racket is normally held with its head up and the racket head slightly on the backhand side of the body. Because most players move forward much better than backward, the base or ready position should be 2–3' back of the middle of the court and astride the center line. In the following discussion of footwork, this ready position will be considered as the middle of the court. (See Figure 6.1.)

Figure 6.1
Ready position.

SWITCH STEP (SCISSORS STEP)

An advanced technique of footwork needs to be learned to deal with all shots that get behind you toward the rear of the court during a rally. This technique is called the "switch step." Using it properly allows you to jump and hit the shuttle as it goes over your head and quickly recover back to the center of the court. A player not developing this technique will experience difficulty in maintaining proper court position.

Figure 6.2A

This technique is used for all forehand or round-the-head overhead shots. As the shuttle starts to go over your head, move toward the rear of the court keeping a sideward position with the left shoulder (right handed player) and hip nearest the net. This position is maintained until the last step is made with the right foot. Jump off the right foot, switch the feet and body position in the air as you strike the shuttle and land on the left foot. As the shuttle is struck, the right shoulder and hip will be

Figure 6.2B

nearest the net. The right foot will be in the air towards the net (somewhere between shoulder and knee-high) for balance as the left foot touches the ground. Push hard off the left foot and recover back to the center of the court. (See Figures 6.2A–D.) This technique is used for clears, drops, and smashes. Many players use this technique with a lot of excess body motion as a form of deception. It is particularly effective when disguising a drop shot that will look like a smash until the last moment.

Figure 6.2C

Figure 6.2D

MOVEMENTS

All of the movements indicated below are for a right handed player.

Movement to the Left Front

For a backhand underhand drop or clear stroke (see Figure 6.3).

1. The first step is a small one toward the left front.
2. The second step is a cross-over step with the right foot. The toes of the right foot will point to the left corner of the net. The weight will be over or even in front of the right foot as the racket moves to a ready-to-hit position. The upper body is bent forward from the waist.
3. The next step can be either a long step with the left foot or a short one, depending on how far you need to go to reach the shuttle.
4. Your last step should always be with the right foot (racket foot). Your weight will shift to the right foot as a backhand underhand drop or clear is made. Your feet will be stretched apart with the left foot closest to the center of the court. The hips will lower as the stretch is made and the shot is executed.
5. To return to the center of the court, push off the right foot and move back to the center of the court with small backward steps. Reassume the ready position.

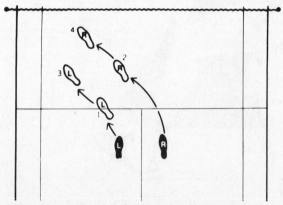

Figure 6.3 *Movement to the left front for a backhand underhand drop or clear stroke.*

Movement to the Right Front

For a forehand underhand drop or clear stroke (see Figure 6.4).

1. The first step is a long one toward the right front.
2. The second step is made with the left foot in a long step toward the right corner of the net. The racket should be moving into the hitting position and the weight is over the front foot with the upper body bent forward from the waist.
3. The next step can be either a long step with the right foot or a shuffle step, depending on how far you need to go to reach the shuttle.
4. Your last step should always be made with the *right* foot (racket foot). Your weight shifts to the right foot as a forehand underhand drop or clear is made. Your foot will be stretched apart with the left foot closest to the center of the court.
5. To return to the center of the court, push off the right foot and move back to the center of the court with small backward steps. Reassume the ready position.

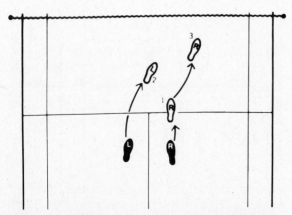

Figure 6.4 *Movement to the right front for a forehand underhand drop or clear stroke.*

Movement to the Left

For a smash return or drive shot on the backhand (see Figure 6.5).

1. The left foot steps back to set up the line of movement. Your weight will be moving toward the left sideline as the left foot moves back. The shoulder begins to turn so that the right shoulder is toward the net and the left shoulder is back.
2. The second step is a cross-over step toward the left sideline with the right foot. Shoulders are parallel with the left sideline as the racket is brought to the hitting position. If necessary for a longer distance, take a shuffle step.
3. Always end with the weight on the right foot as the shot is executed. Your feet will be stretched apart with the left foot closest to the middle of the court.
4. To return to the center of the court, push off the right foot and pivot on the left foot. Adjust your position in the center of the court with small shuffle steps if needed.

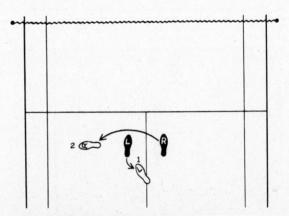

Figure 6.5 *Movement to the left for a smash return or the drive shot on the backhand.*

Movement to the Right

Smash return or drive on the forehand shot (see Figure 6.6).

1. The first step is taken with the right foot. The shoulders turn slightly so that the left shoulder points to the center of the net and the right shoulder points to the back right-hand corner of the court. Your weight should be out in front of the right foot. The knees are bent with the toes of the right foot pointing to the right sideline.

2. The second step is made with the left foot making a shuffle move (left foot moves up to heel of right foot).

3. The last step is always made with the right foot as the racket is brought into hitting position. The feet are stretched apart and the left foot is closest to the center of the court.

4. To return to the center of the court after the shot is executed, push off the right foot and use small shuffle steps to return to the base.

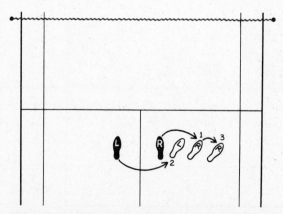

Figure 6.6 *Movement to the right for a smash return or the drive shot on the forehand.*

Movement to the Back Right

For forehand overhead strokes (see Figure 6.7).

1. Pivot quickly on the left foot and step toward the back right corner of the court with the right foot. Shoulders should turn so that the right shoulder points to the back right corner.
2. Second step is a shuffle by the left foot to a spot close to the toe of the right foot. The weight stays as much as possible over the right foot.
3. Continue to shuffle with right and left feet until you are behind the falling shuttle near the back right corner of the court. As shot is executed, the weight shifts from right to the left foot. Hips and shoulders turn so they are parallel with the net as stroke is executed.
4. Take short steps to return to the ready position in the center of the court.

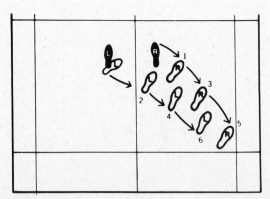

Figure 6.7 *Movement to the back right for the forehand overhead strokes.*

Movement to the Back Left

Backhand strokes (see Figure 6.8).

1. First make a pivot on the right foot and then take a big step with the left toward the back left corner. Try to step as close to the center line as possible to set up the line of movement.
2. The next step is a cross-over long step with the right foot, which sets up the body in the hitting position for the overhead backhand stroke.
3. As you take another left and right step, adjust your movement to the position of the shuttle.
4. The last step should be taken with the right foot and the toes pointing to the left back corner of the court. The weight shifts completely over the right foot as the shot is executed and the back will be pointing to the net.
5. To return to the center of the court, push off the right foot, pivot on the left foot, and take small shuffle steps back to the center of the court. Reassume the ready position.

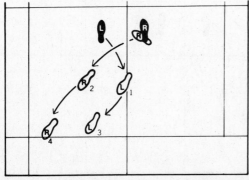

Figure 6.8 *Movement to the back left for the backhand overhead strokes.*

Movement to the Back Left

For round-the-head strokes (see Figure 6.9). This is the same footwork as the *switch step* described earlier in this chapter. Figure 6.2 showed the body position, and Figure 6.9 will show and further describe the position of the feet.

1. First take a small step backward toward the left corner with your left foot.
2. Next take a backward step with the right foot.
3. Continue to take left and right steps backward toward the back left corner until you can reach the shuttle. (Normally it will only take two steps if you are starting from the center of the court.)
4. The last step backward must be a jump upward from the right foot. The shoulders and hips rotate so that the right shoulder and right leg move forward toward the net and the left shoulder points toward the back line. The right foot is lifted in the air for balance. The racket is brought around the head to make the stroke. The stroke is executed while in the air. As you land after the stroke, the weight is completely on the left foot. Push hard off the left foot to regain balance and start back to the center of the court.

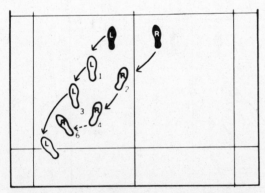

Figure 6.9 *Movement to the back left for round-the-head strokes.*

5. Small steps with the left and right feet are used to return to the center of the court, where the ready position is reassumed.

In conclusion, remember that footwork is essential to get you into proper hitting position. Also remember the *key points of footwork*:

1. Try to get back to base position at center of court between your shots.
2. When reaching center of court, make a jump step and land with feet square and spread at least as wide as your shoulders. This step must be done just *before* your opponent hits the shuttle.
3. *Never* move as your opponent is hitting the shuttle. You can cover a great deal of court in any direction if you are not moving when opponent hits.
4. The last step before you strike the shuttle should always be taken with the right foot (racket foot).

INTERMEDIATE SKILLS

he following intermediate skills have great value when you try to improve your game beyond the beginner level. Each of these skills adds to your repertoire of strokes and poses just a few more problems for your opponent. None of these require any special ability above and beyond the basic skills shown earlier. For example, the drives and round-the-head strokes do not require a change of grip, nor do they require you to hit the shuttle with other than a flat racket. As a matter of fact, the drives are almost identical in the stroke mechanics to the overhead strokes, except that they are played sidearm.

DRIVES

The drive is a flat sidearm stroke which is considered an attacking stroke. It is played on both the forehand and backhand sides and is used more in doubles than in singles play. It is probably used the most in mixed doubles. The contact point for a drive is normally between shoulder and waist height, but it is always hit from as high a position as possible. If hit correctly it will skim close to the net on a line more or less parallel with the floor. (See Figure 5.9 for the proper trajectory.) The shuttle is struck from the side of the body in a flat trajectory with arm extended and racket face pointing toward the net. Use forehand grip for forehand drives and the backhand grip for backhand drives.

Figure 7.1 *Forehand drive.*

Forehand Drives

The forehand drive is played on the right side of the body and is similar to the baseball sidearm throw. If the shuttle is hit close to you, and time permits, you can use a stance with the left foot forward and shift the weight from right to left foot as the stroke is executed. Normally, however, you will need to reach to a sideline to make this shot. If this is the case *always* have your right foot closest to the sideline. This allows you more freedom to execute the stroke and return easily to the center of the court.

As the stance is normally taken with the right foot advanced, the racket is brought behind the back until the racket head is between the shoulder blades. The left shoulder points toward the net. To do this properly, notice that the forearm must bend upward, the wrist must be cocked, and the elbow points toward the ground. (See Figure 7.1.) As the stroke is executed, the elbow will lead the action, which delays the wrist action. At contact point, the following things happen rapidly: (1) the weight should be shifted to the right foot; (2) the body is rotated until at contact point it is facing the net; (3) the arm should be extended; and (4) there should be an inward rotation of forearm and wrist to get maximum timing and power. The arm extension is very similar to the overhead. Try to contact the shuttle to the side and in front of the body (toward the net) when possible. On the follow-through the back of the hand is directly in front of the eyes.

Backhand Drives

This stroke is similar to the forehand side. Right foot is advanced (usually a cross-over) and the racket is brought behind your body. The right shoulder points toward the net as the stance is taken. The elbow is very important in this stroke, as it must be bent and pointing toward the oncoming shuttle. The wrist is cocked with the palm of the hand facing the floor. (See Figure 7.2.) As the shuttle is contacted, the following things happen: (1) weight shifts to the right foot; (2) body is rotated toward the net; (3) arm is straightened; and (4) there should be an outward rotation of the forearm and wrist to get maximum timing and power. The follow-through should be toward the

Figure 7.2 Backhand drive.

path of the shuttle and in the same plane when possible.

Hit the shuttle in front of you (toward the net) when possible.

Cross-Court Drives

There are only three differences in the swing for all cross-court drives. These are: (1) contact *must* be made earlier (at least 12″ to 15″ in front of the body); (2) rotate forearm and wrist strongly and swing hard, for the shuttle must travel several feet further; and (3) follow-through will be across the body rather than straight ahead.

ROUND-THE-HEAD STROKES

The main values of round-the-head strokes are: (1) you can keep the attack by hitting down, whereas backhands are usually more defensive; (2) they can cover for a weak backhand; and (3) a round-the-head attacking shot from the backhand side, such as a cross-court drop or smash, can be a surprise stroke which might upset your opponent. The big disadvantage of a round-the-head stroke is that you may sacrifice court position if you overuse it, for it causes you to take more steps away from the center of the court to play than it does a backhand.

The round-the-head strokes are fairly self-descriptive, for they are forehand overhead strokes played on the left side of the body (the backhand side).

These strokes are usually executed with the forehand grip, although some players prefer to turn the racket more toward the frying pan grip. They feel it is easier to get a flat racket on these shots with this grip. The stroke is closely related to the forehand strokes, except the footwork and body position are quite different. The stroke is started with a forehand stance and the left shoulder pointing toward the net. There is a very quick rotation of the body so that by contact point the right shoulder is pointing toward the net. (See Figure 7.3.) The weight is on the left foot at contact point but the player should strive to move forward quickly to the right foot and return to the center of the court. The racket will come around the head and contact the shuttle on the left side of the body. The back must arch and the knees must bend to make this shot. For best results, the shuttle should be contacted above the left shoulder and not any lower. Most players use a "switch step" to get into hitting position. They will move into hitting position with the left shoulder, hip and foot nearest the net. As the shot is executed, they will jump and exchange feet so that the right foot becomes the one nearest the net. It is from this position in the air that contact with the shuttle is made. As the body lands on the left foot, a hard pushoff is made to shift weight forward and back to the right foot. (See Figure 6.2A–D and Figure 7.3.)

Key Points for Round-the-Head Shots

1. Use a "switch step" just before shuttle is struck.
2. Hit shuttle while it is in the air and right shoulder and hip are nearest net.
3. Land on left foot.
4. Do not use this shot if you cannot recover balance and come back easily to center of the court.

Figure 7.3 *Round-the-head stroke.*

Round-the-Head Clears

At contact point, the racket face points upward and the shuttle is hit to the back of your opponent's court. Most clears of this type are hit straight and not cross-court.

Round-the-Head Drops

At contact point, the racket face points forward toward the net. The shuttle drops just over the net. Either a straight or cross-court drop is very effective, depending upon how your opponent reacts to this stroke.

Round-the-Head Smashes

At contact point, the racket face will point downward. The shuttle must be hit in a downward trajectory. Both straight and cross-court smashes are very effective.

CROSS-COURT NET DROPS

Use the same mechanics for this stroke as for all net strokes. Turn the racket slightly as you start to make the shot (to get proper direction) and stroke the shuttle cross-court. This shot is made both forehand and backhand and must be hit fairly firmly, although very little wrist is used. You must have a good follow-through. Do not jab at the shuttle.

SERVICE RETURNS

Since the service must be made upward, you as a receiver should strive to maintain the offensive. As the forehand is normally the strongest weapon of offense, favor it and take all serves in singles or doubles (with the exception of the low serve to the backhand side) on the forehand. If you are not able to attack the serve, make your return to a spot which will put your opponent in the most difficulty. The receiving stance should be with the weight on the balls of the feet, the left foot advanced, the racket head held about head high, and the player ready to move forward or backward as the serve is delivered. (See Figure 7.4.)

Singles Returns

The stance for receiving singles services should be approximately 5' to 6' behind the short service line, with the left foot closest to the net. Stand next to the center service line in the right court and approximately 3' toward the left sideline in the left court. If your opponent makes a high deep serve, skip sideways to the baseline. Be sure to get behind the shuttle, shift your weight forward to the left foot, and execute your stroke. It doesn't matter whether it is a clear, drop, or smash, although there are some percentage types of returns. These are: (1) if the serve is good and deep, clear straight ahead about 75 percent of the time (this forces your opponent to counter with a good shot); (2) smash only when the serve is not deep; (3) drop occasionally to bring your opponent in, particularly if you have been clearing quite often; and (4) do not use a cross-court very often, as it gives your opponent more time to reach it and opens up wide angles in your defense. (Angles will be discussed later under strategy.)

Doubles Returns

The stance should be the same as in Figure 7.4 with the location about 1' to 3' behind the short service line. The frying pan grip described earlier may be used with great success on your doubles return of service. This

Figure 7.4 *Stance for receiving a doubles service.*

shortened grip allows you to move the racket quicker and perhaps block shuttles that come close to you at a fast pace. This is a very valuable asset in doubles play because the shortness of the court on the doubles serve means that most serves will be low. In doubles, meet the low service ahead of the short service line. Racket head should be up, and inaccurate serves should be hit quickly downward. Even if the serve is good and low, play it with the racket head up. This gives your opponents less time to reach your return and also allows you more possible variety in your shots. By hitting down or flat, you maintain the receiver's offensive advantage.

Figure 7.5 *The* block *return of a smash.*

SMASH RETURNS

Rather than breaking down the smash returns individually, a few general points are all that are necessary. There are three returns to learn when a shuttle has been smashed at you. These are: (1) a straight ahead block (just over the net); (2) a cross-court block; and (3) a straight-ahead half court drive. The first two are the primary returns used in singles, with the latter used quite frequently in doubles. The returns are made on both the forehand and backhand sides. The right foot should be advanced on both strokes if the shuttle is hit down either sideline and not right at you. The shuttle is stroked gently or just *blocked* if the smash has been hit hard. A block entails placing the racket in the path of the shuttle and letting the power of the smash cause the shuttle to rebound over the net. (See Figure 7.5.) On the straight-ahead half court drive, you must hit the shuttle, trying to make it come close to the net as it goes over so that it will land at about the middle of the court down a sideline.

Most beginners have difficulty with the shuttle that is smashed right at the body. There is no set rule on how to defend on these smashes but keep the following points in mind: (1) it is much easier to defend on your backhand against body smashes — you have better range of movement than on the forehand; and (2) try to hit the shuttle as far in front of you as you can — do not allow the shuttle to get too close to you, for it will make your return awkward and usually weak.

ADVANCED SKILLS

There are several strokes in badminton that take a lot of time to perfect before they become a valuable part of your repertoire. Many of those in this chapter may never be learned, but you should at least know they exist. After you have learned the strokes in the chapters on the basic and intermediate skills, you might want to investigate one or more of the strokes in this chapter.

In all the previous strokes the racket face has been flat to the direction of the intended hit. Many of the strokes in this chapter are hit with the racket face at an angle, which produces a sliced shot. This adds a new aspect to the game — deception.

Deception

Deception is a very important part of the game of badminton, for with its use you can out-maneuver your opponent. Perhaps more deception can be used in badminton than in any other racket game because of the rapid deceleration of the shuttle. Some of the ways deception can be used are: (1) by playing the overhead strokes (clear, drop, and smash) from identical motions up to the last second; (2) by using an angled racket face to slice the shuttle left or right (usually a drop shot or half speed smash); (3) by keeping the wrist cocked and pretending to play a drop (holding the shuttle), then, if your opponent goes forward or back, flicking or dropping the shuttle accordingly; (4) by using more or less wrist and forearm rotation to speed up or slow down shots at the last second; (5) by feinting to hit in one direction, then hitting in another (double-motion strokes); and (6) by not overusing a favorite shot or playing in too much of a pattern.

Most deception involves underhand strokes, although you can even hold the shuttle before hitting a clear. An important point about deception and holding a shot is that *it takes time*! You cannot use deception very easily if you are struggling to reach a shuttle. Do not try those feints until you have time to let the shuttle drop before you contact it. Feints or slice shots are very effective against fast opponents who move before the shuttle is struck. By holding and flicking, you can slow their pace and force them to play your style of game.

ADVANCED SERVES

Besides the two basic serves (high deep and short low serves) shown earlier, there are two other serves, used mostly in doubles play, that you should learn. If you mix up your low doubles serve with the following services, your opponents must be alert for any situation.

Drive Serve

The drive serve is a fast, deceptive serve which looks exactly like the low doubles short serve until just before contact. It has a low, flat trajectory that is designed to either pass your opponent or cause him or her to mis-hit the shuttle. The preliminary motion and backswing is exactly the same as the low serve, with a fast rotation of forearm and wrist at contact. Be careful that you do not violate the serving rule. Do not hit the shuttle above the waist. You must, however, be as high as legally possible in order to get the flat trajectory you desire. The best spot to hit the drive serve is at the left shoulder or directly at the face of your opponent.

Flick Serve

The preliminary motions are exactly the same as the low short and drive serves. The main difference is that you will use more wrist action instead of forearm rotation, as little power is needed. The wrist action is used just at contact point to hit the shuttle *just over* your opponent's racket and to the back of the doubles service court. The serve must not be too high or your opponent will get to it easily and smash it. This serve is to keep your opponent honest and not let him or her stand too close to the short service line and rush all your low serves. The best spot to hit the flick serve is wide and deep to the sidelines on the outside of the service area. This forces your opponent to go to the longest distance and allows you more time to get set if he or she is able to smash it.

BACKHAND SMASH

The mechanics of the backhand smash are identical with the backhand clear and drop strokes. The only difference is that at contact point the racket head must be pointing down, as the shuttle must travel downward. Because you cannot hit it as hard as you do the forehand smash, use it only when you are in the front half of your court. Its value lies in being a surprise weapon. The speed of the smash is not always as important as the quickness of the smash, which beats your opponent with its suddenness rather than with power.

ATTACKING CLEAR

The clear that you learned earlier under basic skills was a high clear designed to go deep into your opponent's court and which gave you plenty of time to return to the center of the court. It is sometimes called by the name *defensive clear*.

The attacking clear is not defensive! It is used as another weapon in attacking or keeping pressure on your opponent. Used mostly in singles, its height will vary depending upon the size and speed of your opponent. The shot should go only high enough to clear your opponent's racket and then start to fall. This forces an opponent deep into the backcourt. It is especially valuable on certain types of opponents, some of whom are: (1) short players who must go to the backcourt and catch the shuttle about waist high; (2) slow players who let the shuttle get behind them; and (3) players whose centerbase is on the backhand side of the court to protect their weak backhand. (With these kinds of players, first hit an attacking clear to their forehand; when they hit a weak return from this, attack their backhand.)

I have seen this attacking clear hit as low as 5' or 6' off the ground if the opponent is short. This stroke is a must for a player who hopes to develop a "pressure" type of game and who tries to keep an opponent under constant control. Both kinds of clears are shown in Figure 8.1.

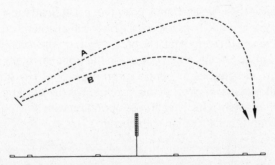

Figure 8.1 *Two kinds of clears:* **A** *represents the defensive high, and* **B** *the attacking low clear.*

ADVANCED DROP SHOTS

The drop shot explained earlier under basic skills is what we consider a slow drop. It travels slightly upward off the racket face. It should land inside the short service line and be hit with a flat face. There are also two other drops which should be mentioned under advanced skills; these are the fast drop and the cut drop.

Fast Drop

This drop is hit quite a bit harder than the slow one (almost like a slow smash). It should barely clear the net and land beyond the short service line up to 3' or 4' toward the backcourt area. This shot is hit either with a flat face or a sliced partially opened face. Its main values are: (1) in doubles or mixed doubles where a slow drop would be killed by a person at the net; (2) to get the shuttle on the floor fast in singles (if your opponent is off-balance or out of position); and (3) as a surprise shot to keep your opponent guessing. (See Figure 8.2 for the differences in the two drops.)

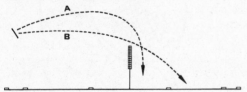

Figure 8.2 *Two kinds of drops:* **A** *represents the slow, and* **B** *the fast drop.*

Cut Drop

This is a fast drop and should not float across the net. The racket face is partially opened to slice the shuttle. The main values in using this drop are: (1) it is very deceptive as it looks like a straight ahead clear; (2) it gets to the floor fast; and (3) with practice you can control it as well as or better than a straight drop. This slice can be either right to left or left to right.

HALF-SMASH

The mechanics are identical with those for the forehand smash in the chapter on basic skills. The half-smash is so called because it has less speed and lands closer to the net. Its chief values are: (1) it does not pull you out of position — after you hit it, it is easier to return to the center of the court; (2) it is played with less effort, so it does not tire you as quickly; (3) it is good for use against an opponent out of position — it gets to the floor fast (very good for cross-court smashes); and (4) if you are an attacking type of player, it keeps the attack. This stroke can be made with a flat face or a partially opened face (slice). The latter is usually used for this shot. This is used quite frequently in singles and mixed — not as often in regular doubles.

Figure 8.3 *The brush return of a tight net shot.*

BRUSH RETURN OF TIGHT NET SHOTS

This shot is very valuable when your opponent has played a drop shot from the net which comes over to your right side of the court only 2″ to 3″ above the net. If you hit in the direction of the net to put it away, you can easily hit the net. Instead, use the forehand side of your racket and swing in the same direction as the net (right to left) and brush (or slice) across the shuttle. (See Figure 8.3.shot will stay in the court because you have taken the speed off the shuttle with the slicing motion. By swinging in the same direction as the net, you also eliminate the possibility of hitting the net, which is a fault. This shot can also be hit on the backhand side of your racket when the shuttle comes over to your left side of the court. The backhand seems to be a more difficult shot for most people, so practice it first on the forehand.

This shot is also valuable in returning a good low serve in doubles. You must catch it at tape level and hit it toward the back opponent on the other team. The brushing action of the shot is deceptive, as it appears to your opponent that you are hitting the shuttle to his or her right, while in reality it comes to the left.

difference between : doubles & singles

TACTICS AND STRATEGY

There is no one way to play the game of badminton. Every year new champions are developing their own successful methods of play. There are, however, general tactics that might benefit most players whether they play a powerful (attacking) game or a running type of game. In general: (1) be prepared to change your style of play if it is losing; (2) do not change a winning style; (3) develop a killer instinct— beat your opponent as quickly as possible; (4) avoid playing your opponent's game — force him or her to play yours; (5) know that you are fit — this gives you confidence that your opponent cannot "just outrun you"; (6) develop the ability to concentrate and think all the time you are playing a match; and (7) be a champion in defeat as well as victory.

This chapter will be divided into two parts so that players can progress at their own pace. The first section will discuss basic strategy for singles, doubles, and mixed, and will be followed by a section on advanced strategy.

BASIC STRATEGY

This section will be devoted to the basic tactics that a beginning player should learn to utilize. Be sure you know the following material well before progressing to the section on advanced strategy.

SINGLES

Singles is a game of patience, fitness, and court position. Essentially, the basic strategy is to maneuver your opponent up and back by a series of drops and clears until he or she makes a weak shot or an error. Only then do you look to smash for an outright point. Remember that the smash is to finish rallies and not to force openings. If you smash too much it will tire you out, particularly if you are smashing from too deep in the court. Then your opponent can easily defend on your smash and turn it into an offensive shot by cross-dropping your smash. It doesn't take very much thought to determine why you run your opponent up and back instead of from side to side. The singles court is only 17' across, whereas the court is 22' long from the net to the baseline. You can run your opponent even further if you make him or her move diagonally, for then the court becomes approximately 28' long.

It is extremely important in badminton to develop shots for both offensive and defensive play. In every game (perhaps every point of a game), your position will change from offense to defense or vice versa. *Offensive* strokes are those which force an opening or are hit downward, such as smashes, half-speed smashes, drop shots, low serves, and low attacking clears. *Defensive* strokes are those which give your opponent the attack and are usually hit upward, such as high clears (both overhand and underhand), high serves, and underhand drop shots. Drive strokes can be either offensive or defensive, depending on whether they force an opening (offensive) or are hit upward when they cross the net (defensive).

Early in your career you must determine what type of game you expect to play. Are you going to be an attacker, a defensive player, or a combination of the two? Once you make this decision (have a good player or coach help you make it when possible), work on those strokes which are best suited to your particular style. For example, a defensive player would work on high serves, high clears (both underhand and overhand), and slow drops. An attacking player would work more on a mixture of high and low serves, flat fast clears, fast drops, and also hard half-speed cut smashes.

Serve

The main serve in singles should be the high, deep serve. Try to hit the serve so it drops straight down close to the back line, as this forces your opponent deep and, because of the angle, is very difficult to time. Many players will mis-hit the shuttle for this reason. If your opponent is stroking well and giving you difficult shots to reach off your deep serve, it would be worthwhile to try a few low, short serves to upset your opponent's rhythm. For the most part, hit the deep serve close to the center line of the receiving court, since this narrows the possible angle of return (see Figure 9.1). Vary this serve with

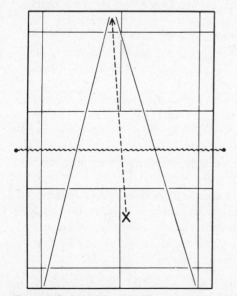

Figure 9.1 *A deep singles serve to the middle to narrow angle of return.*

occasional serves to the outside corners, but remember, this widens the angle of return. Angle of return will be discussed more fully in the advanced section.

Your serving position should be about 3′ to 6′ back of the short service line and next to the center line. After serving, one step will move you into the center of your court. This is your normal base. Your ready position should be assumed with both feet spread at least the width of the shoulders and square to the net.

Service Returns

Your receiving position will be about 6′ behind the short service line. In the right court you will be near the center line, whereas in the left court you will be 3′ to 4′ to the left of it. Be in a diagonal stance with your left foot advanced, as it is easier to move up and back in this position.

If your opponent's serve is high and deep, your best return is a straight ahead clear to the opposite baseline. Occasionally you might vary this with a straight ahead drop shot. Stay away from cross-court returns off the serve unless your opponent has a very weak backhand, in which case you might clear cross-court to the backhand. If your opponent's serve is high but *short* of the 2½′ doubles service line, you can use a variety of returns, such as: (1) smash; (2) cross or straight drop; or (3) fast attacking clear.

If your opponent serves you low, two returns are the most efficient and least risky: (1) a straight drop played close to the net; and (2) a flick straight clear if opponent starts to move toward the net shot. Always meet the low serve as soon as possible, as this puts more pressure on your opponent.

Do not play too close to the lines in your opening points of the game, as you can make errors. Instead, keep a safe margin inside the lines so as not to present your opponents with gift points. Make them earn each one by putting the shuttle on the floor on your side.

Smash Returns

The best return of a smash in singles is a drop shot

(sometimes called a block) to the net. If your opponent has smashed from relatively deep in the court, play your drop about 6" to 8" above the net so the shuttle will loop. This will force your opponent all the way into the net and can turn his or her attacking stroke into a forcing shot for you. If time permits, play your drop cross-court. This only holds true if an opponent has smashed straight. If smashed cross-court, play a straight drop. These two drops hit away from your opponent will create problems: (1) time — less time for opponent to play the next shot; and (2) distance — opponent must cover more distance before hitting the next shuttle.

General Play

Remember, it was mentioned earlier that your basic shots will be drops and clears to maneuver your opponents up and back in the court. Keep them on the move. Opponents are more likely to make errors if they must stroke while moving than if they are standing still and hitting.

After every stroke the player should return to the base in the center of the court and be ready for the next shot. This is not always so easy to do. If your shot is a bad one or if your opponent gets to your shot before you can get back to your base, *stop* wherever you are just before your opponent hits the shuttle. Never be moving as he or she strokes, for you can be too easily faked and fooled. It is surprising how much court you can cover if you stop until the shuttle is struck by your opponent and then move, for you rarely *false step*, that is, take a step in the wrong direction.

When you get into trouble, hit a high deep clear. This gives you more time to get back to your base and helps relieve the pressure your opponent may be applying to you. This high clear can be hit both underhand or overhand and forehand or backhand.

DOUBLES (MEN OR WOMEN)

There are three formations that a team might use. These are: (1) sides, (2) up-and-back, and (3) combination. Only the first two will be covered here, as the combination will come under the advanced section in this chapter.

BASIC FORMATIONS

Sides

This formation is probably the easiest to teach beginners (see Figure 9.2). The court is divided down the middle and each player covers their half from the net to the baseline. The serving and receiving positions on the serve are also side-by-side as during play. The advantages of this are: (1) each player's area is definitely marked and little confusion results which could cause missed shots or broken rackets; (2) it is simple and easy to learn; and (3) it is a good defensive formation and very difficult for opponents to smash through. Unfortunately, the disadvantages may outweigh the advantages of this formation. These disadvantages are: (1) a smart team will play only on weaker players, running them up and back in their half of the court; and (2) you cannot attack effectively from this formation. Remember this: *attack* is

Figure 9.2

the key in doubles! You cannot beat most teams if you do
not attack them.

Up-and-Back

This formation is usually used in two ways: (1) if one
partner is quite a bit stronger than the other, the weaker
one plays net and the stronger one covers all the
backcourt; or (2) if a team wants to try to attack at all
times. The court is divided into front and back court and
each player covers one half. (See Figure 9.3.) It is easy
and simple to learn and clearly defines each player's
responsibilities. The team starts up-and-back and the
server follows a low serve in to the net and stays there.
The partner covers the backcourt. Its big disadvantage is
that the opponents can run the back player from side to
side, and it is impossible for that person to cover smashes
down both sidelines. This is obviously a weak defensive
formation. The main advantages are: (1) the ability to
attack well from this formation; and (2) the ability to *hide*
a weaker player at the net.

Figure 9.3

BASIC FUNDAMENTALS

There are certain fundamentals which are basic to both of the above formations. These will be covered now, with advanced theories coming later.

Service

The low service is the basic serve in doubles. You do not win very many outright points with it, but it causes your opponents to hit the shuttle up where you can start your attack. The best spot for the low serve is close to the center line, for this narrows the angle of return. In the up-and-back formation, the server must step forward after serving and cover all net strokes. In the sides formation, each partner would cover his side of the court from the baseline to the net.

The flick serve is the main weapon used to offset the opponents rushing your low serve. This serve has been described in Chapter 8. It can be effective when hit either close to the center line or wide to the alley (sometimes called tramlines). In the up-and-back formation, if the server flicks, that player still goes to the net. The net player covers only the drop shots, while the other partner will take all smashes or clears. In the sides formation, both partners cover their normal halves of the court on the flick serve.

Service Returns

The receiver stands one to three paces back of the short service line. The stance is covered in Chapter 7. The shuttle must be taken early as it crosses the net and the racket head must be up. Only in this manner can you put pressure on the serving team. Try to return the service with a close drop shot or a push shot down the closest sideline. Avoid cross-court returns, for they widen the area your team must cover. If the serve is high, the receiver should smash the shuttle straight ahead. If not on balance, the receiver should play a fast drop straight ahead.

Smash

The mechanics of the smash are covered in Chapter

5. The position or placement of the smash is very important. Never try to smash cross-court in doubles, as the shuttle decelerates very rapidly as it continues in flight, and your opponent's return can give you difficulty. Your smash should be straight (as a general rule) and to the inside of the player straight ahead. This will usually give him or her more difficulty in driving the shuttle cross-court where it could hurt you. Another main advantage of smashing in this area is that your partner knows where you are hitting and can anticipate your opponent's return.

Drop

The mechanics of the drop are covered in Chapter 5. In doubles, the drop should not be hit slow, for one of the opponents could anticipate it and kill it. Usually the drop is hit to the center of the court. There are three reasons for using this spot: (1) it cuts down the angle of return; (2) it is easier for your partner to cover the net if you drop in the middle; and (3) you may confuse your opponents as to which one of them is to play the shuttle.

Smash Return

The mechanics of the smash return are covered in Chapter 7. There are three standard returns of good smashes: (1) a straight ahead drive, (2) a straight ahead drop shot, and (3) a cross-court clear. The disadvantage of the cross-court clear is that it takes very good timing and still leaves you on the defensive. It will be discussed more fully under advanced strategy. The best return of a smash is usually a straight ahead drive down the closest sideline. The straight drive must be hit fairly close to the net and down the alley so that the opponent who covers the net cannot reach it and hit it downward. It must also be hard enough to carry at least past the short service line. This forces the opponent who is in the backcourt to hit it around waist or knee high. That player cannot make a strong attacking stroke from this low position, but will play a drop shot to the middle or a flat drive. Either of these should be fairly easy for your team to handle.

If the opponent at the net moves back too deep to try and reach this half court return, you should play a drop shot, either straight or cross-court. The straight drop is safer, usually more effective, and also easier to hit. If you do hit this drop, it is imperative that you follow your shot to the net so that your opponents must hit the shuttle upward, which gives your team the attack.

MIXED DOUBLES

As a general rule, mixed doubles is played in a manner very similar to the up-and-back formation described under doubles. The man covers all of the backcourt while the woman covers the net. This formation is maintained at all times, if possible. The woman will stand on the short service line during play and during the man's service. The side she stands on during service will depend upon whether her partner is left- or right-handed. (If he is right-handed, she stands on the left side.) Of course, if a man and woman are of comparable skill, they can play in regular doubles formation.

Serve

The short serve is used most of the time. The woman serves from about one pace back of the short service line and follows the serve in to cover all net strokes. The man serves from three to four paces back of the short service line. He does not follow his serve in but stays back and covers all the backcourt. Services will usually be low and to the center of the court, which narrows the angle of return. Because the woman stands closer to the net when serving, the opponents have less time to see the shuttle when playing their return. For this reason most of the points in mixed doubles result from the woman's service.

Occasional flick serves are good for keeping your opponents honest. They are especially effective in serving to many women for, even if they get to your service, they cannot smash it through you.

Service Returns

This is a very important skill in doubles or mixed. You must attack the serve to put your opponents under pressure. The receiving stance is described in Chapter 7.

Because he must cover the back two-thirds of the court, the man must rush the serve more cautiously in mixed. His two best returns are: (1) drop shot in front of his own partner, or (2) a half court push shot down the closest sideline just past the opposing woman at the net. This forces the opposing man to hit up on his next shot. The woman receiving service can make either a net shot (usually straight) or a half court push just past the opposing woman. Both players should avoid slow returns to the center of the court which the opposing man can drive fast and deep to either corner.

Any high serve or flick serve should be smashed if possible. As a general rule, smash straight ahead down the alley or tramlines. This forces the man to cover the side and hit the shuttle upward. If a drop shot must be made, hit a fast drop straight down the side. Avoid the center of the court with your drop, for the opposing woman should be there to kill any weak drops.

Smash

All smashes in mixed are generally directed down the sidelines, as your opponents are normally up-and-back. More important than speed in your smash is the trajectory. Hit the shuttle down at a sharp angle. Then if it comes back, it must come up to you and you keep the attack. If you do not wish to smash down the sideline, smash downward with a sharp angle at the woman or between the opposing players. The smash at the woman is usually effective as she is near the net and has less time to react to the smash than her partner.

Drop

As mentioned on service returns, all drops must be fast ones directed down the sidelines away from the center of the court. The man must be careful of drops because he is usually hitting from the back court, and a slow drop can be killed by the opposing woman. For this reason, he normally plays half court push shots past the woman instead of drops. The woman at the net must be able to hold her own playing drop shots with the opposing woman. She should only hit cross-court drops when the opposing woman is pulled over to one sideline.

Drives

Drive mechanics are covered in Chapter 7. The drive strokes are used more in doubles than any other game. Be careful of the cross-court drives. They are probably *overused* rather than underused. Only use this stroke when the opposing players are both pulled to one sideline. Other than the above, keep your drives straight and down the sideline.

Smash Returns

In basic mixed strategy, the woman would duck all smashes and cover only net shots. Later, in the advanced section, she will aid her partner when protecting against a smash. Normally the man will defend against the smash in mixed from about 5 or 6 paces back of the short service line. He tries to keep his return flat and straight down the closest sideline. If he can hit it half court just behind the opposing woman, well and good. But if he cannot, he hits it hard and flat so that the opposing man gets it lower than the net and cannot smash it again. Occasionally, your opponent's smash can be driven cross-court if he has smashed off balance or from too deep in his court.

ADVANCED STRATEGY

This section will be devoted to skills involving more than the basics described earlier. Remember, badminton is a game which requires you to *think* if you expect ever to be a champion.

Learn to concentrate on each point in the game and try not to give any points away without your opponent earning them. Use the warmup session and the first few points of a match to determine what kind of players you are facing. Are they slow afoot? Are they erratic? Is their deep backhand weak? Do they overplay so much to cover their backhand that they open up their forehand corner? Can you beat your opponent with quick shots? If there is a weakness, find it! Try to win every tournament match with a minimum of effort, saving that energy for those tough matches that will come later.

Warmup

In many tournaments you cannot take 10 to 15 minutes for a warmup, so do some limbering up exercises before you go to the court for your match. Start with shoulder and arm rotations and slowly work down until you have stretched the back and leg muscles thoroughly (see Chapter 10). This will prevent pulled muscles and get you ready to play. During the warmup rallies, aim for specific spots when you stroke so you start gaining the accuracy needed at the outset. Practice the specific strokes which will be needed for the game you are about to play (for example, clears and drops in singles; smashes, drops, and defense in men's doubles; drives for the man and net shots for the woman in mixed doubles). Scout your future opponents if time permits. Note whether they are left-handed, like to run, smash hard, and so on.

Advanced Singles

Practice Every time you go on the court for practice, use your brain. Have a definite goal in mind for each training session. For example, if your smash defense is weak, clear short to your opponent and let him or her smash. This will give you valuable practice in returning smashes and your opponent does not need to know you are practicing. If you have a partner who will practice with you, well and good. If everyone says, "I do not like to practice, let's play games," do not despair. Use the games to practice certain skills. Occasionally play a game without using one of your basic strokes (clear, drop, or smash). Use only the other two and try to win. This gives you valuable training. Drills that you can use with a willing partner will be discussed in Chapter 11.

In practice, work on hitting the two types of clears: (1) a defensive (high) clear, and (2) an attacking (low) clear. Practice playing one game with all defensive clears. Then play another game and use only attacking clears. Spend a lot of time and effort on perfecting your *length* in the clears. This one item probably causes more losses than any other skill — the inability to hit a good clear that will consistently land within 6″ of the back line.

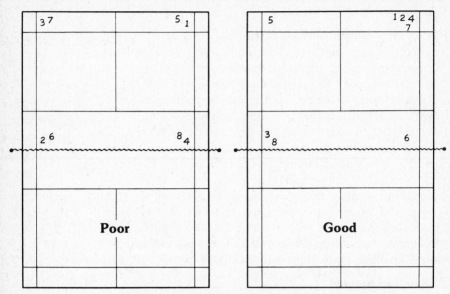

Figure 9.4 Poor *and* good *variety in singles pattern.*

Avoid Stereotyped Play Be sure you do not get into a stereotyped pattern which your opponent can anticipate. Figure 9.4 shows poor and good variety. Instead, play two, three, or four shots in a row to the same corner.

A Conditioned Response A good sequence to use against some players is what is called the *conditioned* pattern. Hit four, five, or six shots to one spot and then with the same motion, to disguise your intentions, hit to the diagonally opposite corner. (See Figure 9.5.) After you have hit four or five to one corner your opponent may get conditioned to this shot and take a step in that direction as you prepare to stroke again. The shot to the opposite corner will beat him or her.

Center Court Theory A good strategy to use at the end of a game involves the center court theory. Let's say the score is 12–12, 10–13, 9–14 (and you are tied or losing), and you are faced with the problem of trying to completely eliminate all errors from your game. Under this system you do not hit shots close to a sideline.

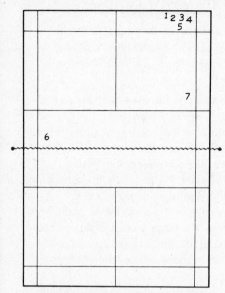

Figure 9.5 *A pattern to achieve a conditioned response.*

Figure 9.6 *Target area for body smashes.*

Primarily you try to smash a lot, using body smashes against your opponent. Change the pace of your smash and change the position you try to attack. If you must clear or drop, hit into the center of the court. This eliminates most errors and narrows the angles open to your opponent.

   Body Smashes These are underused by most good players. Most players defend well against sideline smashes, for they are reaching and have full use of the arm and racket. A smash into the body, however, will often cramp their return and force them to hit a drop short or a pop up. As most players carry their rackets slightly on the backhand side, your target should be the right side of the opponent's body. (See Figure 9.6.) If you hit a good smash, move to the net and hit a weak return which usually results. If your opponent is able to hit a good drop, there is nothing lost, for you are at the net and ready to play your return anyway.

   Half-Speed Smashing This skill is very valuable in singles. This is the primary smash to hit on all cross-courts, because it forces your opponent to move forward to play this shot or be beaten by the angle. Remember that a hard smash will carry the shuttle much deeper in the opposite court. See Figure 9.7 for a combination of hard and cut smashes.

The Power Game If you have a strong smash and are reasonably quick, you might want to try this type of game. Learn to get the attack as soon as possible in a rally and continue to attack until you win the point. The key word with this style of play is *pressure*. Get your opponents under pressure and keep them there until they crack. Besides the high deep serve, two others are important for a power player: (1) a low serve, and (2) a flick deep singles serve. The latter is used while you are successfully maintaining the attack with a low service. This deep serve variation keeps your opponent from rushing your low service.

On every occasion when you want to clear *and* are on balance, use the low attacking clear. This shot, if properly

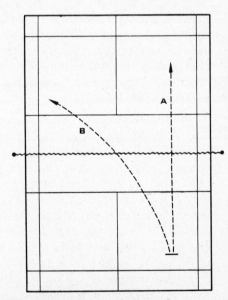

Figure 9.7 *Two different kinds of smashes:* A *represents the hard, and* B *the half speed or sliced smash.*

executed, gets the shuttle behind your opponent, who must then lift the shuttle to you. See Chapter 6 for the mechanics of this stroke, which should usually be played straight ahead. It doesn't matter whether you hit it to the forehand or backhand side of your opponent. Ideally, it should be hit within 6" to 1' from the singles sideline. This prevents opponents from jumping and intercepting your shot which they might do if hit too close to the middle of the court.

A hard smash is very helpful with this style of play, but more important is proper placement of the smash. Learn to smash straight, cross-court, and into your opponent's body. Varying these three smashes creates more problems for your opponent. The half-speed smash is a necessity with the above hard smash, for there are numerous occasions when you want to attack but are too deep in the court or are off-balance and the hard smash would hurt your court position. Use the half-speed smash on these occasions and keep the attack. The great value of this half-speed smash is the steep angle and trajectory that forces your opponent to come forward in the court to reach it.

Most drop shots should be fairly fast ones so they get below the level of the net quickly. This forces your opponent to hit up. It does not matter if the shuttle carries a little past the short service line on this fast drop.

To play a really good attacking game, you must also develop a good net game. Make your opponents afraid to play net with you. If they are deep in the court and have hit a drop shot, play your return about 5" above the net and let it come down close to the net. (See Figure 5.9.) This forces your opponents all the way into the net. If they clear from this position, they will not normally be able to get the shuttle deep. If they do clear short, *attack* with your smashes.

Work to get a weak return that you can kill. If you are unable to kill the shuttle when you are at the net, push it quickly into your opponent's body. This usually elicits a weaker return that you can kill.

Angle of Return The angle of return is the angle through which your opponent can hit the shuttle. In singles, you try to do two things: (1) narrow the angle to which your opponent can hit, and (2) widen the angle to which you can hit. The easiest method of studying angle of return is on the serve. If you serve from next to the center line of your court to a spot close to the center line of your opponent's court, you narrow the angle and equalize the danger on either side. Your opponent must hit away from you to try and pass you. (See Figure 9.1.)

If you serve deep and to the sideline, you widen the angle of return. You must cover the straight ahead shot down the line possibility first, but you are then left vulnerable to the cross-court shot. After a serve such as this, move 2' or 3' to the left. Now you are *centrally* in the angle of return. This angle of return holds true on all shots, but it is much harder to adapt your position during a rally than during the serve.

Court Position Court position will vary depending upon what shot you have hit, the possible angle of return, and what alternatives your opponents have in their selection. For example, if you have hit a good close drop shot and your opponent must come from the backcourt to retrieve it, do not run back to your central base! Wait at the net and, if they play a net return and it is high, kill it! If they clear, it almost certainly must be short. You will have plenty of time to walk back to half court and smash it.

Many times you can eliminate one or two spots to which your opponent cannot hit. When this happens, vary your court position so as to be close to the probable returns.

Advanced Doubles (Men or Women)

The best formation to play in doubles is a mixture of the sides and up-and-back formations. This is called a Combination (or rotation) System. Because it takes extremely good teamwork, advanced skills are necessary to make it work. This system has simple rules for court positions. They are: (1) when the shuttle is up in the air and you are attacking, be in an up-and-back formation; (2) when the shuttle must be hit up by your team, adopt a sides formation so you can defend. As you can see, your team will be making a constant change (or rotation) from sides to up-and-back and from up-and-back to sides, depending upon the situation. Figure 9.8 shows how this is done most efficiently.

If either player should clear the shuttle while in the attacking formation, the team immediately assumes sides. Since the back line player can see the net player coming back, he or she assumes the opposite side from that which the net player chooses. Normally the net person would come straight back or the opposite side of the clear.

The same change of formation must occur when the defensive team gets a high shuttle and starts to attack. The player away from the shuttle goes to the net, and the player who is closest moves over to smash or drop.

If the shuttle is lifted only to midcourt, it is best if the strikers move forward to the net after hitting it down. This is best for several reasons: (1) they are usually moving forward when they hit anyway; (2) they are moving and thus more ready for the next shot; and (3) since they hit the last shot, they should have a good idea of the opponent's reply.

Services Reread the material on drive, flick, and low serves in Chapters 5 and 7. As mentioned earlier in this

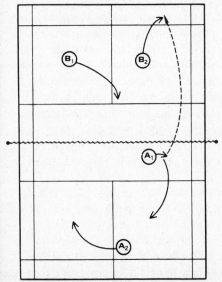

Figure 9.8 Combination formation in doubles.

chapter, the basic serve in doubles is low. Because most good players will stand close to the short service line and move across just as soon as the shuttle is struck, however, your low service must be varied in placement. Even this may not be good enough against a good net rusher. You must use a deceptive flick or drive serve to fool your opponent, who will not be able to rush as effectively if you have flicked or drive-served successfully. The preliminary motions of the low, drive, and flick serves must look exactly the same. The proper mechanics of these strokes are covered in Chapters 5 and 7.

As previously mentioned, vary the placement of your low serve. Three spots are effective! (1) The *best* spot is always closest to the inside of the opponent's playing court next to the center service line. This narrows the angle of your opponent's return. (2) Another good service placement is wide to the alley. This is effective against some people who do not move or change direction well. Many times the opponents will push this serve deep. If you have served from the left court it allows your partner to drive the return fast and hard. (3) A third spot is your opponent's left shoulder if received with the racket held on the forehand side, as most players do! If received with the racket on the backhand side, serve to the right shoulder. This spot is very good against an opponent who has difficulty changing the racket from one side to the other. Many times a player will have a moment of indecision as to which side of the racket to use to play the shuttle, and will eventually hit a weak return.

The drive serve is valuable against players with slow reactions. It is usually served right at the face of your opponent or to his or her left shoulder. *Avoid* this serve (to the left shoulder) if your opponent hits a good around-the-head smash.

The flick serve is made to one of the two following areas: (1) to the outside of the court in the alleys; or (2) to the inside of the service court next to the center service line. Both serves have certain advantages. The serve to the outside takes longer for the opponent to reach, thus giving your team more time to get set for the return. If an opponent smashes cross-court, the server has a slower shot to react to than if the serve is to the inside and a smash is played straight ahead. The advantage of the serve to the inside is that it is to your opponent's backhand side and he or she may be unable to smash around-the-head, but may have to hit up, which immediately gives your team the attack.

Advanced Service Returns As mentioned earlier, hit the shuttle as soon after it crosses the net as possible. You should learn several varied service returns. This puts extreme pressure on your opponents just to get the shuttle back over the net, which takes their minds off attacking you. The better returns of service are: (1) a half-court push, usually straight, just past the server but in front of the partner, (2) a straight drive deep to the box in the back corner, (3) a drop shot away from the server, (4) a push shot into the server's partner aimed about chest high on the forehand side (if that player defends on the backhand), and (5) a push shot just over the back of the server, who usually steps forward while serving to cover the net. Two other returns are very effective if the serve is delivered low to the outside alley: (1) a push shot cross-court straight into the server who is moving to cover the serve, and (2) a half-court straight push shot off the serve. This shot should be past the server but in front of the partner. Should your opponents flick serve you, hit a half-speed smash straight ahead. This shot will give the opponents trouble, for it has good trajectory and does not leave you off balance. A drive serve by your opponents should be smashed back at the server or blocked quickly over the net toward the middle of the court.

Advanced Smashing The best placement of a smash is *always* to the inside of the player straight ahead, as mentioned in basic strategy. The main reasons for this are: (1) it is more difficult for an opponent to hit a hard cross-court drive, which could hurt you; (2) the straight smash gets to the opponents quicker; and (3) your partner knows where you are smashing and is able to anticipate certain returns from the opponent. Because most players defend better on the backhand, some teams prefer always to smash to the opponent's right side. They feel this forces a weaker return, particularly if the smash is kept close to the opponent's right hip.

If you encounter opponents who are defending well against your smash, change the spot of your attack to alternating sides (such as forehand to backhand to forehand to backhand). This forces them to alter their position on each of your smashes. If they retreat deeper in the court to have more time on your smashes, use a steep angled smash with a little less power. This shot may hit the floor in front of their outstretched rackets. Vary the speed of your smashes. Occasionally hit a flat, slow smash into your opponent's chest area. This may change his or her timing and rhythm, particularly if he or she is having success against your hard smash. If your opponent moves toward the center of the court to defend, smash down the alleys. This is particularly good if you first smash one down the middle of the court to open up this area.

If your opponents lift the shuttle down the center of the court, smash down the center line. This is good for a couple of reasons: (1) indecision may cause neither player to hit the shuttle; and (2) the angle of the opponent's return cannot give you great difficulty as could a sideline smash. *You win in good doubles by smashing.*

Advanced Drops The basic strategy section covered this area well. The drop is used in doubles for: (1) deception, (2) to gain (or regain) your balance, and (3) as a variation from smashing.

Advanced Smash Returns The straight ahead drive and straight drop shot returns were covered in the basic strategy section. Three other returns are used frequently in doubles. They are: (1) a cross-court drive, (2) a straight or cross-court clear, and (3) a cross-court drop shot. The cross-court drive is particularly effective when your opponents are both shifted to one side of the court. Be sure to contact the shuttle well out in front of the body when you make this shot. The cross-court drop is also used if your opponents are both shifted to one side of the court and anticipating a straight drive or drop. Remember that this shot is risky if hit too slowly, for it takes longer to cross the net. You must follow this shot to the net as it is hit in order to force the opponents to hit the shuttle upward. If you are at the net, they will be fearful of playing a return drop which you might kill. The straight or cross-court clear must be timed correctly to consistently return a smash to the back area of the opponent's court. If both you and your partner are good on defense and feel that you might tire the attackers and win in this manner, this could be the style for you. Hit the shuttle well in front of you and be aware of possible changes in shuttle speed, for mistiming can ruin your deep defensive return.

What happens if you are the player cross-court from the smasher? We know that as a general rule the attacking team works on the player straight ahead. As the cross-court player, you must cover smashes to the inside down the middle. Ordinarily you try to hit two returns. These are: (1) a block or drop back to the same side as the smasher, with your partner following it to the net, or (2) a straight drive down your closest sideline. If this straight

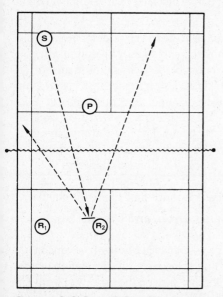

Figure 9.9 *Smash returns by the cross-court defender.*

drive gets past the opponent at the net, it will win a rally outright or force the smasher to make a long run to retrieve it. If the opponent does reach it, he or she will probably have to hit the shuttle upward, which will give your team the attack. (See Figure 9.9 for these two returns.)

Advanced Mixed Doubles

Advanced Services This was covered well in basic strategy. An occasional drive serve or low serve into the left shoulder is also effective. This low serve may cause a moment of indecision regarding use of the forehand or backhand side of the racket to hit the shuttle. In the basic section, it was noted that the woman stands on the short service line when the man serves, and to his *left*, if he is right-handed. Many men, however, will ask the woman to stand on the same side to which they are serving. It is felt that this gives their team better position in case the opponents hit a straight drop. The man must be careful to give the opponents a good look at the service and not unsight them with a partial blocking of the shuttle by the woman's position.

Advanced Service Returns Besides the two basic service returns of the drop shot or the half-court push, there are three other possible service returns in mixed doubles: (1) A straight flat drive into the "box" where the two side and end lines converge, (2) A push into the man's chest (often cut across slightly to take the speed off the shuttle), made by the man if he has a strong partner who can play behind him so he can rush the net, and (3) A short half-court shot played just over the server's shoulder. **Caution** — Use (3) only against the woman's serve, for the man has too much time to see the shuttle.

Advanced Smash, Drop, and Drives These strokes were covered well in the basic section on mixed doubles. The only problem which ensues in advanced mixed is the up-and-and back defensive formation where the woman covers the smashes on the side away from the smasher. (See Figure 9.10.) This formation poses a problem for the attackers, for if they smash straight ahead, the opposing man is set for the shot. If they attack the woman with the slower cross-court smash, it may be picked off and blocked down the opposite sideline. Then what can they do? If smashing is not successful (try it first), try steeply angled smashes to the body or the left shoulder of the woman. If this does not work, use straight drops to bring the man in, mixed occasionally with flat attacking clears over the woman's head, which may cause problems for the opposing man. You should also try smashing or dropping down the center to see if this poses a problem of who will play the shot. Every defense has a weakness — keep probing until you find it!

Advanced Smash Returns As mentioned earlier, the man tries to defend against his opponent's smash with a straight ahead half-court drive. It must go over the net low and close to the sideline so the opposing woman cannot reach it. This takes the attack away from the opponents. Occasionally, if the woman moves over to try to cut off one of these half-court drives, a cross-court

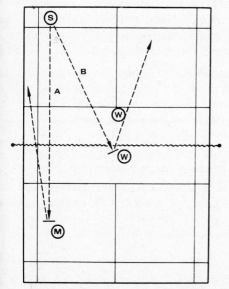

Figure 9.10 *Smash returns of an up-and-back mixed doubles team: A (man) blocks smash straight to one-half court, B (woman) blocks smash down opposite sideline.*

block to the net is very effective. It must not be too slow or the woman can recover and still hit it down.

The woman can help defend against smashes by the opposing man in two ways: (1) cover all of one side as in regular doubles; (2) cover all smashes directly at her on the side opposite to where the smash has been struck. This last formation needs a little explanation. Teams that use this defensive formation, sometimes called a *diagonal defense*, try always to clear down a sideline. This gives the woman time to get cross-court away from the shuttle. The woman stands in front of the short service line with her racket head up. She covers only smashes or drops directly to her side, with the man covering all the other areas. Her partner would cover the straight drops, straight smashes, and clears to his or her side of the court. (See Figure 9.10.)

When the man smashes cross-court at the woman, she blocks the shuttle straight ahead. It will usually go half-court past the opposing woman and give the man considerable difficulty. The reason the woman can cover this shot effectively is that the smash hit cross-court must be hit further, and therefore reaches her with a little slower pace than would a straight smash.

Strategy During Play The woman hits all shots downward, when possible, at the net. She takes a very short backswing on shots and tries for kills or half-court push shots when possible. She tries not to reach behind her body to play a shot, for usually the man is in better position as he has more time. If the woman does reach back, she usually hits a weak return. She must be a very accurate net player and have the confidence to play the opposing woman at the net. She keeps these shots straight unless the opposing woman has been pulled to one side of the court, in which case a cross-court drop can safely be played.

The man in mixed doubles will usually hit about two-thirds of the shot because he is covering the back two-thirds of the court.

He keeps the shuttle flat (or downward) when possible with half-court drives. If the opposing man gets to your half-court fast and is giving you considerable difficulty with his returns, play deep into the corner boxes. This gives him less time to fake. The woman plays only one-third of the court but it's the toughest position. She constantly has to make decisions about whether to attempt a shot or let the shuttle go past her to her partner. (As there is no one behind the man, he doesn't have this problem!) The woman has the toughest position and will normally put away more shots than her partner. His shots are usually designed to create openings for his partner at the net to kill the shuttle and end the rally. Much of the strategy is designed to get the opponents to clear so a team can attack with smashes. Anytime the opportunity presents itself, a team should *smash*, for this will win in doubles and mixed.

If you play against a mixed doubles team that plays the sides formation, attack them like regular doubles by hitting your smashes and drops down the middle.

CONDITIONING

This chapter is mainly for those players who want to compete in tournament play. Several of the previous chapters have been devoted to developing badminton strokes and learning strategy. You must also train to become physically fit if you expect to become a top player, since strokes are useless without the conditioning that must also be developed. There are two types of conditioning that will be discussed in this chapter: (1) general conditioning for overall fitness, and (2) specific conditioning for badminton.

GENERAL CONDITIONING

One of the best methods of developing overall conditioning for any sport is *running*. Little equipment is required and there are always open areas such as school tracks, fields, and streets on which to run. If you are completely out of condition, start slowly and jog only one lap (or two minutes) the first time out. Slowly increase your distance until you can run two miles in 12–14 minutes. When you can run two or more miles and recover in a few minutes without excessive discomfort, your general conditioning is good and distance running should be used just for maintaining your overall condition. You are now ready to progress to specific conditioning for badminton. Although I have never personally believed in it, some competitive players run 5–6 miles a day. If it works for you, do it!

SPECIFIC CONDITIONING FOR BADMINTON

Players get tired in badminton from quick starts, stops, and changes of direction. Specific conditioning, then, should consist mainly of quick bursts of speed and many changes of direction. Use as many gamelike drills as possible. Many of the drills in Chapter 11 can be modified to work on strokes and conditioning and are excellent. I favor conditioning work *on the court* with gamelike drills whenever possible.

Below are a few drills to give you an idea of what movements can be stressed. Keep an account of the number you do of each in one minute (or 5 minutes). Strive to set new records each time you exercise.

Alternate Foot Touch

Stand on singles and doubles sideline (facing the court) with one foot on the singles and the other on the doubles sideline. Alternate feet on each line by jumping and exchanging feet as rapidly as possible. How many can you do in 30 seconds? In one minute? Increase this drill until you can do it for five minutes.

Click Feet Together

Stand on the deep doubles service line and the

baseline with one foot on each line. Jump and click feet together once and then return feet to the same lines. How many can you do in 30 seconds? In one minute? Increase this drill until you can do it for five minutes.

Shuttle Pickup #1

Place one shuttle on each of the doubles sidelines. Starting with a shuttle in your hand, run alternately to each side of the court and exchange the shuttle in your hand with the one on the floor. How many can you do in one minute? In five minutes?

Shuttle Pickup #2

Place 10 shuttles on the right singles sideline. Starting in the center of the court, run to the right sideline and pick up one shuttle. Reverse direction and run to the left sideline and place the shuttle on the floor. Repeat until all the shuttles are placed on the left sideline. (Note: Footwork should be stressed by taking the last step with your racket foot as the shuttle is either picked up or placed on the floor. Keep opposite foot as close to the center of the court as possible and stretch out to pick up or release shuttle. Push off racket foot to return to opposite sideline.) When this drill becomes too easy, increase the number of shuttles. This drill can be run to either side.

Line Touch

On a badminton court (without a net), start at one baseline and run to the short service line, touch the line with one hand and return to the baseline; next, run to the short service line on the opposite side of the court, touch line and return to the baseline; next, run to opposite baseline, touch and return; then run to opposite short service line and to baseline. How long does it take you to do this entire run? Try to shorten your time as much as possible on future runs.

Sprints

(Do these on a track or in a gymnasium.) Run forward or backward for twenty yards. Then walk for twenty yards and repeat. Try to accelerate as quickly as possible. Do several of these sprints until you get tired. Increase the number of sprints every day.

Shadow Badminton

Stand in the middle of a badminton court and run to all corners of the court playing an imaginary rally (hit clears, drops, and smashes). Return to the center of the court after each imaginary stroke. Work on good footwork during this drill as you tend to do what you practice.

Make your drill more difficult by having a friend stand in the middle of the net and point to different corners. This makes the drill more realistic as you do not know the location of your next move, just as you do not know the location of your opponent's next shot in an actual game.

There are other drills that could be used which are just as good as the ones presented. There are a few that I have seen used effectively in the development of tournament players of championship caliber. Stress the following items when developing conditioning drills: (1) keep them as gamelike as possible; and (2) work on quick starts, stops, and changes of direction as these factors cause you to tire when playing an opponent of equal or better skill.

DRILLS AND GAMES

This chapter will be divided into two sections: basic drills and games, and advanced drills and games. This is done so players can progress at their own pace. Once the basic section has been conquered adequately, move on to the advanced.

Why spend time on practice which could be spent playing games? Psychology has shown us that overlearning needs to take place before a person can execute motor skills correctly. You must practice a particular skill until it becomes a part of your neuromuscular pattern. The racket must feel natural in your hand, and the contact between the racket head and the shuttle must be coordinated to permit good timing and proper stroking.

BASIC

Overhead Clear Drill

Both players (A and B), as illustrated in Figure 11.1A, start from the center of the court, with A using a deep singles serve to get the rally going. B clears it back with an overhead clear. The object is to clear the shuttle high and deep back and forth across the net. Work first on straight clears and use only forehand or round-the-head overhead strokes. After you become proficient at hitting forehands, work also on the overhead backhands. Once you are able to clear straight consistently to within 1′ of the back line, then work on cross-court clears along with the straight ones. Because of the increased distance when you hit cross-court, be sure to hit the shuttle harder.

Overhead Dropshot and Underhand Clear Drill

Both players (A and B), as illustrated in Figure 11.1B, start in the center of the court. A starts the rally by a deep serve and B returns the serve with an overhand drop shot, trying to keep the shuttle inside the short service line on the opponent's side of the court. A will move forward and return this drop with a high clear, trying to get the shuttle within 1′ of the baseline. Usually both A and B hit to one particular corner until some degree of accuracy is attained, and then the spot is shifted. After both players achieve success in overhand dropping (forehand and backhand) and underhand clearing (forehand and backhand), then you can increase the difficulty of this drill by having A drop to either side and by having B underhand clear to either side. Both players should return to their center position to make the drill more realistic and closely related to a game situation. (Player who makes the underhand clear can practice footwork with this drill at the same time.)

Straight Drive Drill

Both players (*A* and *B*), as illustrated in Figure 11.1C, start in the center position. *A* starts off with a predetermined drive serve to *B*'s forehand or backhand. *B* should drive the shuttle flat and straight down the side. If *A* hits to *B*'s forehand, and *B* hits a straight drive, this will be followed by a backhand drive by *A*. *Keep the shuttle straight* until the shuttle can be hit repeatedly with direction and control. Cross-courts will be discussed later.

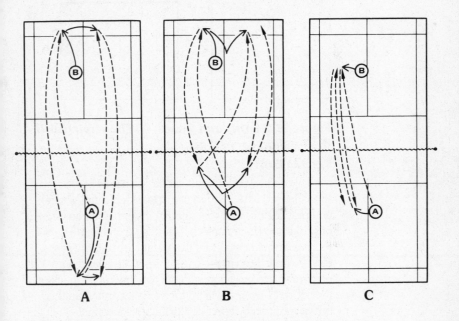

Figure 11.1 Drills: A. *The overhead clear.* B. *The overhead drop shot and underhand clear.* C. *The straight drive.*

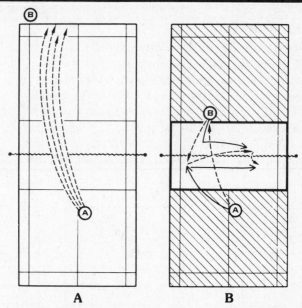

Figure 11.2 *Drills and games:* **A.** *The serving drill.*
B. *The short (or net) game.*

Serving Drill

This drill can be utilized with a partner or by oneself.
(See Figure 11.2A.) Try to use at least ten shuttles when
you practice this skill so a definite rhythm and consistency
of stroke can be perfected. If working with a partner, the
receiver should always let the shuttle drop so the server
can see how deep in the court the shuttle is landing. Work
on getting it to land between the two lines at the back of
the court. Later you will try for a smaller area than this,
but get your serve consistently into this area first.

Short (or Net) Game

This game is played between the two short service
lines, with the exception of the initial serve. (See Figure
11.2B.) The initial serve must be a normal low doubles
service into the proper court. Score exactly like singles
and play a regular game. The sideline can be either the
singles or doubles lines. This game has value not only in
teaching scoring but also in developing your touch on
straight and cross-court shots. Any shot which goes past
the short service line is out of court and loses the rally.

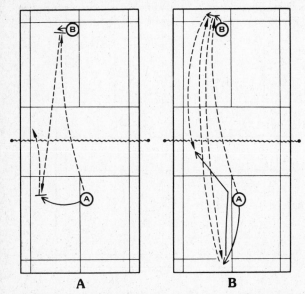

A　　　　　　　　　　**B**

Figure 11.3 *Drills:* **A.** *The smash and drop (block).*
B. *The overhand clear and drop combination.*

Smash and Drop (Block) Drill

This drill is valuable for teaching the smash and
defense against a smash. (See Figure 11.3A.) Player *A*
serves high to about three-quarter court. *B* hits a
predetermined straight or cross smash which *A* blocks
back over the net. By using 20 or so shuttles, more
practice can be accomplished in a short period of time.

Overhand Clear and Drop Combination Drill

This drill is valuable in teaching the player to use the
preliminary windup for both the overhand clear and drop
shots. (See Figure 11.3B.) Player *A* will serve high and
deep to player *B*, who hits a deep clear followed by a
drop shot. Player *A* will return all of *B*'s shots with a high
clear as *B* alternates hitting a clear, drop, clear, drop. After
several minutes of this, players change positions and
player *A* does the clearing and dropping.

Smash and Half-Court Drive Drill

This drill is valuable for teaching the smash and basic

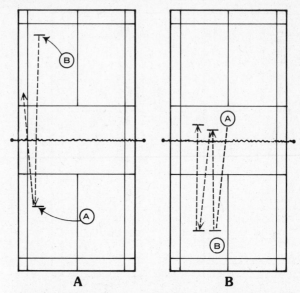

Figure 11.4 *Drills:* **A. Smash and half-court drive.**
B. *Overhead push and drive.*

smash defense for doubles play. (See Figure 11.4A.)
Player A high serves to three-quarter court. B hits a
straight smash which A drives to half court straight ahead.
A serves a new shuttle. If A starts with 10–20 shuttles,
both players get a lot of practice in a short period of time.

Overhead Push and Drive Drill

This drill is designed to practice two skills for doubles
play. (See Figure 11.4B.) These skills are: (1) Overhead
pushes from net — racket up by player A (similar to
Figure 7.4), standing between net and short service line,
and hitting hard push shots directly at player B; (2)
Smash defense — Player B (in stance similar to Figure
6.1), standing 2–3 feet from deep doubles service line
toward net, hits Player A's push shots back toward net
with a short quick flat stroke. Player B tries to keep the
shuttle as near to the top of the net as possible when
hitting the shuttle toward Player A. The object of the drill
is to keep the rally going with quickness and with hard
shots crossing the net within 2–6 inches of the top of
the net.

ADVANCED

Half-Court Singles Game

This game is valuable in teaching the player to run the opponent up and back in the court. (See Figure 11.5A.) The court is divided down the middle by an imaginary line which continues the middle line all the way across the court. Play a regular game and keep score. The only difference is that you would serve straight ahead and not diagonally, as must be done in a proper game. A certain amount of control is necessary before the players can utilize this game efficiently.

Smash-Drop-Clear Drill

This drill is good for working on three skills at one time. (See Figure 11.5B.) For this reason it is beyond the basic drills and included in the advanced. Player A serves high to three-quarter court area for B to smash. A returns B's smash with a drop which B clears and A smashes.

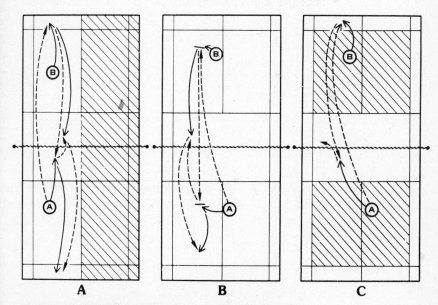

      A   B   C

Figure 11.5 *Drills and games:* **A.** *The half-court singles game.* **B.** *The smash-drop-clear drill.* **C.** *The long and short game.*

The drill is continued in this manner, with the shuttle being smashed-dropped-cleared by both players until one player makes an error. The position of the smash can be predetermined at first until both players develop the ability to return each other's smash.

Long and Short Game

This game is played and scored like regular singles, except control of the shots is stressed. (See Figure 11.5C.) Every clear must be hit within the two lines at the back of the court, and all drops must be hit inside the short service line and the net. Any clear or drop not landing in their respective areas are not hit back over the net. This forces each player to concentrate on hitting *deep* clears and *short* drops and avoid playing strokes into the center of the opponent's court.

Singles Court vs. Baseline Game

This is a very good game to use if the two players are not equal in playing ability. (See Figure 11.6A.) The good

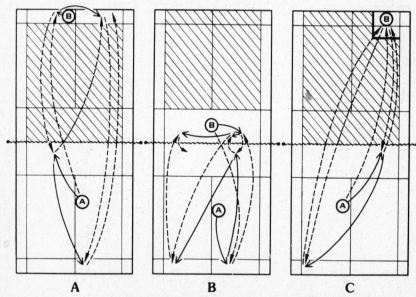

A   B   C

Figure 11.6 *Drills and games:* **A.** *The singles court versus the baseline game.* **B.** *Alternating drop-clear drill.* **C.** *The uneven partner's game.*

player *A* is allowed to hit *only* within the last 2½′ of the court (between doubles service line and baseline), while the weak player *B* can hit anywhere within the singles court. No matter what shot is hit, *A* must hit the shuttle deep to the back of *B*'s court. The only exception is if *B* hits such a weak return that it would usually be smashed by an opponent. If this happens, *A* can smash but must hit the smash within 1′ of either sideline. Regular score is kept.

Alternating Drop-Clear Drill

This is a very good drill for learning to hit on the move and also for conditioning. (See Figure 11.6B.) It can also be used to give a better player a good workout against a weaker player. If *A* is to be the runner, that player will hit nothing but drop shots to either side of the court. Player *B* will alternate hitting a drop followed by hitting an underhand clear. (Example: *B* serves deep — *A* overhand drops — *B* redrops — *A* redrops — *B* clears — *A* overhand drops — *B* redrops — *A* redrops — *B* clears.) If you can follow this example, you will find that *A* does all the running by dropping from deep court followed by running to the net and redropping and then back to the baseline for another overhand drop. *B*, on the other hand, stands at the net and drops to pull *A* into the net; this is followed with an underhand clear to push *A* deep in the court.

Uneven Partners Game

This is a very good game to use when two players are uneven in skill. (See Figure 11.6C.) Strong player *A* picks out one of the four corners of the court to which all strokes in the rally must be hit. Weak player *B* may hit to any spot on the court that person chooses. This is great for helping *A* to develop conditioning and also the ability to hit any shuttle to a specific spot on the court. Player *B* gets the opportunity to use all the strokes without moving excessively and thus practices control. This can be scored like a regular game or just used as a drill.

Smash, Block, and Drop Drill

This drill can be used to practice strokes but also is

super for working on *conditioning and quickness*. (See Figure 11.7A.) Player *A* hits a high serve two-thirds deep in even court followed by *B* hitting a straight smash down *A*'s backhand side. *A* replies with a straight block (drop) to net which is followed by *B* hitting a redrop at net. *A* straight clears to two-thirds court and drill continues. (Note: This drill can be run on one-half the court and same drill by other players on other side. Player *A* can increase the speed between shots that are hit to Player *B* which helps that player to develop quickness. Extending each rally to 20 or more smashes for Player *B* helps to develop conditioning. Player *A* should keep 3–4 shuttles in hand to restart a rally immediately if either player misses a shot.)

Smash and Half-Court Drive Drill

This drill is designed to practice smashes and drives which are the basic smash defense for doubles. (See Figure 11.7B.) Player *A* high serves to three-quarter court. Player *B* hits a straight smash which *A* drives to half-court straight ahead and close to sideline. Player *B* returns this drive with a drop shot close to net. Player *A* clears this drop to three-quarter court and drill is repeated. (Note: Player *B* does all the smashing and *A* all

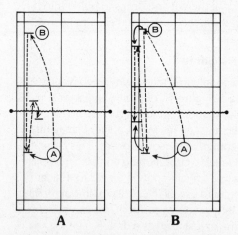

A   **B**

Figure 11.7 *Drills*: A. *Smash, Block, and Drop*. B. *Smash and Half-Court Drive*.

the defending.) This drill can be used as a conditioner by speeding up the shots and keeping the rallies going for 20 or more smashes.

Smash, Drop, and Cross Clear Drill

This drill is designed to practice smashing while on the move. (See Figure 11.8.) Player A high serves to even court about two-thirds deep. Player B smashes straight down singles sideline aiming for the sideline. Player A returns this smash with a backhand straight drop. Player B follows with a cross-court clear about two-thirds court deep. Player A moves over and hits a straight smash down B's backhand side aiming for the sideline. Player B returns this smash with a backhand straight drop. Player A hits a cross-court clear off the forehand side and the drill is repeated. (Note: This drill can also be done in two additional ways. These are: (1) Player A high serves to odd court and B hits round-the-head straight smash; A follows with a straight drop; B then hits a cross-court clear; A follows this with a round-the-head straight smash or (2) A high serves to even court and B hits cross-court smash; A then drops straight and B hits a straight clear; B hits cross-court smash and A follows with a straight drop.)

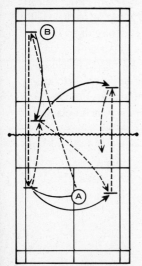

Figure 11.8 *Drills: Smash, drop, and cross clear.*

Doubles Drill for Four Players

This drill is designed to improve doubles skills with all four players on the court. (See Figure 11.9.) Players A and B are partners and are practicing the "defensive phase" of doubles. Players C and D are on the offensive and are practicing the "attacking phase" of doubles. Players A or B start the rally by serving high to player D. Player D smashes at either of the defending players (usually straight) who return the smash with a straight flat drive down the nearest sideline. (In Figure 11.9, B has served high to D who smashes straight and B replies with a straight drive down the nearest sideline. Player B *must* keep the return out of the middle of the court where player C can reach and attack the return. (Player C smashes all weak returns.) Player B's drive return is followed by a drop shot by player D anywhere at the net. Either A or B return D's drop shot with a high underhand clear that should be hit to the opposite corner away from player D to make that person run to get the return. Player D moves over quickly and smashes straight to player A who replies with a straight drive and the drill continues. (Note: As players become more skilled, variations are added. Some of these are: (1) Player D can either smash or drop from backcourt with A or B replying to drop with a cross-court clear; (2) Player A or B can reply to D's smash with a drive or drop close to net [straight or cross-court]. As mentioned earlier, player C kills all weak returns in middle of court or at the net. If unable to kill, player C drops the shuttle at net and either A or B [whoever is closest] clears to corner away from player D.)

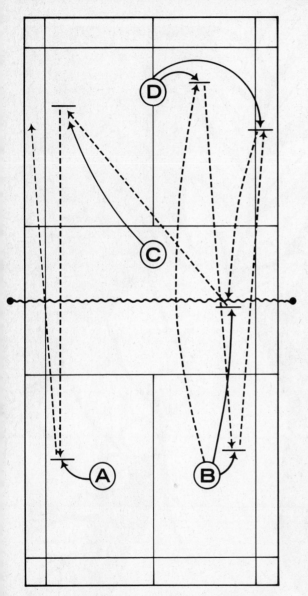

Figure 11.9. *Drills: Doubles Drill For Four Players.*

ACCOMPLISHMENTS

Who are the top American players today and throughout the past several years? Who are the top international players? Which countries win the Thomas Cup? The Uber Cup? These questions are continually being asked the author by beginning players and interested people. This chapter is devoted to answering these questions by listing the best players in this country since World War II, the winners of the All-England Championships, and the Thomas and Uber Cup International Team Champions. The winners of the All-England are usually considered to be the unofficial world champions by most badminton authorities.

As mentioned previously in Chapter 1, the United States has had two truly outstanding world champions: Dave Freeman and Judy Devlin Hashman. Dave was undefeated in singles from 1939 through 1953 and also won several men's doubles and mixed doubles championships. Judy won 31 U.S. national titles and 17 All-England titles since 1954. Other Americans who have outstanding records include the following:

Jim Poole (total of 46 No. 1 rankings or senior championships) — U. S. No. 1 in men's doubles with Don Paup for eleven years, No. 1 in mixed doubles for two years, and No. 1 in men's doubles with Mike Walker for two years. Besides these twenty-three No. 1 rankings, Jim has also won twenty-three senior championships since 1972 including the last ten straight in men's singles. Jim also has won ten Canadian open or senior championships and the Malaysian singles championship in 1961. (Jim Poole and Erland Kops of Denmark are the *only* non-Orientals to win this prestigious title.)

Wynn Rogers (total of thirty-eight No. 1 rankings or senior championships) — Seventeen years No. 1 in men's doubles with Joe Alston (14) and two other partners; eight years No. 1 in mixed doubles with five different partners and also eight senior championships since 1961.

Ethel Marshall (total of twenty-nine No. 1 rankings or senior championships) — U. S. No. 1 in singles for seven years, two doubles with Bea Massman and three mixed doubles with Bob Williams. Ethel also won sixteen senior and master championships.

Joe Alston (total of twenty-six No. 1 rankings) — U. S. No. 1 in singles for five years, fourteen years No. 1 in doubles with Rogers, and seven years No. 1 in mixed with his wife, Lois.

Don Paup (total of eighteen No. 1 rankings or senior championships) — U. S. No. 1 in men's doubles for 11 years with Jim Poole and one year with Bruce Pontow, U. S. No. 1 in mixed doubles for two years with Helen Tibbetts. Don has also won four senior championships since 1979.

Pam Stockton Brady (total of seventeen No. 1

rankings) — U. S. No. 1 in singles for five years, No. 1 in doubles for seven years, and No. 1 in mixed for five years.

Bea Massman (total of fourteen No. 1 or senior championships) — U. S. No. 1 in women's doubles for two years and twelve senior and master championships.

Helen Tibbetts (total of eleven No. 1 or senior championships) — U. S. No. 1 in women's doubles for two years and No. 1 for three years in mixed doubles. Helen has also won six senior and master championships.

Tyna Barinaga (total of eleven No. 1 rankings) — U. S. No. 1 in singles for three years, No. 1 in doubles for six years, and No. 1 in mixed for two years.

Mike Walker (total of nine No. 1 rankings) — U. S. No. 1 in singles for one year, No. 1 in doubles for three years, and No. 1 in mixed four five years.

Lois Alston (total of nine No. 1 rankings or senior championships) — U. S. No. 1 in doubles for one year and U. S. No. 1 in mixed for seven years. Lois has also won one senior championship.

Judianne Kelly (total of nine No. 1 rankings)—U. S. No. 1 in singles for one year. No. 1 in doubles for three years, and No. 1 in mixed for five years.

Chris Kinard (total of seven No. 1 rankings) — U. S. No. 1 in singles for seven years.

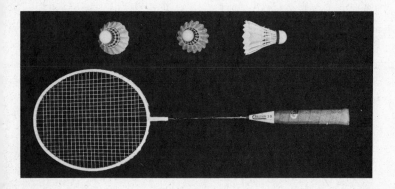

Listed below are the U. S., All-England, and International Team Champions.

U. S. NATIONAL RANKINGS (1947–81)

Men's Singles	Women's Singles	Men's Doubles
1947 D. Freeman	1947 E. Marshall	1947 D. Freeman-W. Kimball
1948 D. Freeman	1948 E. Marshall	1948 D. Freeman-W. Rogers
1949 D. Freeman	1949 E. Marshall	1949 W. Rogers-B. McCay
1950 M. Mendez	1950 E. Marshall	1950 W. Rogers-B. McCay
1951 J. Alston	1951 E. Marshall	1951 J. Alston-W. Rogers
1952 M. Mendez	1952 E. Marshall	1952 J. Alston-W. Rogers
1953 D. Freeman	1953 E. Marshall	1953 J. Alston-W. Rogers
1954 J. Alston	1954 M. Varner	1954 J. Alston-W. Rogers
1955 J. Alston	1955 J. Devlin	1955 J. Alston-W. Rogers
1956 J. Alston	1956 J. Devlin	1956 J. Alston-W. Rogers
1957 J. Alston	1957 J. Devlin	1957 J. Alston-W. Rogers
1958 R. Palmer	1958 J. Devlin	1958 J. Alston-W. Rogers
1959 J. Poole	1959 J. Devlin	1959 J. Alston-W. Rogers
1960 J. Poole	1960 J. Devlin	1960 J. Alston-W. Rogers
1961 J. Poole	1961 J. Devlin Hashman	1961 J. Alston-W. Rogers
1962 J. Poole	1962 J. Devlin Hashman	1962 J. Alston-W. Rogers
1963 J. Poole	1963 J. Devlin Hashman	1963 J. Alston-W. Rogers
1964 C. Ratanaseangsuang	1964 D. O'Neil	1964 J. Alston-W. Rogers
1965 C. Ratanaseangsuang	1965 J. Devlin Hashman	1965 J. Poole-D. Paup
1966 J. Poole	1966 J. Devlin Hashman	1966 J. Poole-D. Paup
1967 J. Poole	1967 J. Devlin Hashman	1967 J. Poole-D. Paup
1968 J. Poole	1968 T. Barinaga	1968 J. Poole-D. Paup
1969 S. Hales	1969 T. Barinaga	1969 J. Poole-D. Paup
1970 R. Starkey	1970 T. Barinaga	1970 J. Poole-D. Paup
1971 R. Starkey/S. Hales	1971 D. Hales	1971 J. Poole-D. Paup
1972 C. Kinard	1972 P. Stockton	1972 J. Poole-D. Paup
1973 C. Kinard	1973 P. Stockton	1973 J. Poole-D. Paup
1974 C. Kinard	1974 C. Baker	1974 J. Poole-D. Paup
1975 M. Adams	1975 J. Kelly	1975 J. Poole-D. Paup
1976 C. Kinard	1976 P. Stockton Bristol	1976 D. Paup-B. Pontow
1977 C. Kinard	1977 P. Stockton Bristol	1977 J. Poole-M. Walker
1978 M. Walker	1978 C. Carton	1978 J. Britton-C. Coakley
1979 C. Kinard	1979 P. Stockton Brady	1979 J. Poole-M. Walker
1980 G. Higgins	1980 C. Carton	1980 M. Fogarty-M. Walker
1981 C. Kinard	1981 U. Kinard	1981 G. Higgins-J. Britton

Women's Doubles	Mixed Doubles
1947 J. Wright-T. Scovil	1947 W. Rogers-V. Hill
1948 J. Wright-T. Scovil	1948 C. Stephens-P. Stephens
1949 J. Wright-T. Scovil	1949 W. Rogers-L. Smith
1950 J. Wright-T. Scovil	1950 W. Rogers-L. Smith
1951 D. Hann-L. Smith	1951 W. Rogers-L. Smith
1952 E. Marshall-B. Massman	1952 W. Rogers-H. Tibbetts
1953 J. Devlin-S. Devlin	1953 J. Alston-L. Alston
1954 J. Devlin-S. Devlin	1954 W. Rogers-D. Hann
1955 J. Devlin-S. Devlin	1955 J. Alston-L. Alston
1956 E. Marshall-B. Massman	1956 B. Williams-E. Marshall
1957 J. Devlin-S. Devlin	1957 B. Williams-E. Marshall
1958 J. Devlin-S. Devlin	1958 B. Williams-E. Marshall
1959 J. Devlin-S. Devlin	1959 M. Roche-J. Devlin
1960 J. Devlin-S. Devlin	1960 M. Roche-J. Devlin
1961 J. Devlin Hashman-S. Devlin Peard	1961 W. Rogers-J. Devlin Hashman
1962 J. Devlin Hashman-P. Stephens	1962 W. Rogers-J. Devlin Hashman
1963 L. Alston-D. Haase	1963 J. Alston-L. Alston
1964 T. Barinaga-C. Jensen	1964 J. Alston-L. Alston
1965 T. Barinaga-C. Jensen	1965 J. Alston-L. Alston
1966 T. Barinaga-C. Jensen	1966 J. Alston-L. Alston
1967 J. Devlin Hashman-R. Junes	1967 J. Alston-L. Alston
1968 T. Barinaga-H. Tibbetts	1968 L. Saben-C. Starkey
1969 T. Barinaga-H. Tibbetts	1969 D. Paup-H. Tibbetts
1970 T. Barinaga-C. Jensen Hein	1970 J. Poole-T. Barinaga
1971 C. Jensen Hein-C. Starkey	1971 J. Poole-M. Brecknell/D. Paup-
1972 P. Stockton-P. Bretzke	H. Tibbets
1973 P. Stockton Bristol-D. Hales	1972 T. Carmichael-P. Stockton
1974 P. Stockton Bristol-D. Hales	1973 T. Carmichael-P. Stockton Bristol
1975 C. Starkey-D. Hales	1974 M. Walker-J. Kelly
1976 P. Stockton Bristol-R. Lemon	1975 M. Walker-J. Kelly
1977 D. Osterhues-J. Wilts	1976 M. Walker-J. Kelly
1978 D. Osterhues-J. Wilts	1977 B. Pontow-P. Stockton Bristol
1979 P. Stockton Brady-J. Kelly	1978 B. Pontow-P. Stockton Bristol
1980 P. Stockton Brady-J. Kelly	1979 M. Walker-J. Kelly
1981 P. Stockton Brady-J. Kelly	1980 M. Walker-J. Kelly
	1981 D. Brady-P. Stockton Brady

ALL-ENGLAND CHAMPIONSHIPS (1947-80)

Men's Singles	Men's Doubles
1947 C. Jepsen (Sweden)	1947 T. Madsen-P. Holm (Denmark)
1948 J. Skaarup (Denmark)	1948 P. Dabelsteen-B. Frederiksen (Denmark)
1949 D. Freeman (U.S.A.)	1949 Ooi Teik Hock-Teoh Seng Khoon (Malaya)
1950 Wong Pen Soon (Malaya)	1950 P. Dabelsteen-J. Skaarup (Denmark)
1951 Wong Pen Soon (Malaya)	1951 E. Choong-E. B. Choong (Malaya)
1952 Wong Pen Soon (Malaya)	1952 E. L. Choong-E. B. Choong (Malaya)
1953 E. Choong (Malaya)	1953 E. L. Choong-E. B. Choong (Malaya)
1954 E. Choong (Malaya)	1954 Ooi Teik Hock-Ong Poh Lim (Malaya)
1955 Wong Pen Soon (Malaya)	1955 F. Kobbero-J. Hansen (Denmark)
1956 E. Choong (Malaya)	1956 F. Kobbero-J. Hansen (Denmark)
1957 E. Choong (Malaya)	1957 J. Alston (U.S.A.)-H. Heah (Malaya)
1958 E. Kops (Denmark)	1958 E. Kops-E. Nielsen (Denmark)
1959 Tan Joe Hok (Indonesia)	1959 Lim Say Hup-Teh Kew San (Malaya)
1960 E. Kops (Denmark)	1960 F. Kobbero-E. Nielsen (Denmark)
1961 E. Kops (Denmark)	1961 F. Kobbero-J. Hansen (Denmark)
1962 E. Kops (Denmark)	1962 F. Kobbero-J. Hansen (Denmark)
1963 E. Kops (Denmark)	1963 F. Kobbero-J. Hansen (Denmark)
1964 K. Nielson (Denmark)	1964 F. Kobbero-J. Hansen (Denmark)
1965 E. Kops (Denmark)	1965 Ng Boon Bee-Tan Yee Kahn (Malaysia)
1966 Tan Aik Hunag (Malaysia)	1966 Ng Boon Bee-Tan Kee Kahn (Malaysia)
1967 E. Kops (Denmark)	1967 H. Borch-E. Kops (Denmark)
1968 R. Hartono (Indonesia)	1968 H. Borch-E. Kops (Denmark)
1969 R. Hartono (Indonesia)	1969 H. Borch-E. Kops (Denmark)
1970 R. Hartono (Indonesia)	1970 T. Bacher-P. Petersen (Denmark)
1971 R. Hartono (Indonesia)	1971 Ng Boon Bee-P. Gunalan (Malaysia)
1972 R. Hartono (Indonesia)	1972 Christian-Ade Chandra (Indonesia)
1973 R. Hartono (Indonesia)	1973 Christian-Ade Chandra (Indonesia)
1974 R. Hartono (Indonesia)	1974 Tjun Tjun-Wahjudi (Indonesia)
1975 S. Pri (Denmark)	1975 Tjun Tjun-Wahjudi (Indonesia)
1976 R. Hartono (Indonesia)	1976 B. Froman-T. Kihlstrom (Sweden)
1977 F. Delfs (Denmark)	1977 Tjun Tjun-Wahjudi (Indonesia)
1978 Liem Swie King (Indonesia)	1978 Tjun Tjun-Wahjudi (Indonesia)
1979 Liem Swie King (Indonesia)	1979 Tjun Tjun-Wahjudi (Indonesia)
1980 P. Padukone (India)	1980 Tjun Tjun-Wahjudi (Indonesia)

Women's Singles

1947 M. Ussing (Denmark)
1948 K. Thorndahl (Denmark)
1949 A. Schiott Jacobsen
         (Denmark)
1950 T. Ahm (Denmark)
1951 A. Jacobsen (Denmark)
1952 T. Ahm (Denmark)
1953 M. Ussing (Denmark)
1954 J. Devlin (U.S.A.)
1955 M. Varner (U.S.A.)
1956 M. Varner (U.S.A.)
1957 J. Devlin (U.S.A.)
1958 J. Devlin (U.S.A.)
1959 H. M. Ward (England)
1960 J. Devlin (U.S.A.)
1961 J. Devlin Hashman (U.S.A.)
1962 J. Devlin Hashman (U.S.A.)
1963 J. Devlin Hashman (U.S.A.)
1964 J. Devlin Hashman (U.S.A.)
1965 U. Smith (England)
1966 J. Devlin Hashman (U.S.A.)
1967 J. Devlin Hashman (U.S.A.)
1968 E. Twedberg (Sweden)
1969 H. Yuki (Japan)
1970 E. Takenaka (Japan)
1971 E. Twedberg (Sweden)
1972 N. Takagi (Japan)
1973 M. Beck (England)
1974 H. Yuki (Japan)
1975 H. Yuki (Japan)
1976 G. Perrin Gilks (England)
1977 H. Yuki (Japan)
1978 G. Perrin Gilks (England)
1979 L. Koppen (Denmark)
1980 L. Koppen (Denmark)

Women's Doubles

1947 K. Thorndahl-T. Olsen (Denmark)
1948 K. Thorndahl-G. Ahm (Denmark)
1949 H. Uber-Q. Allen (England)
1950 K. Thorndahl-G. Ahm (Denmark)
1951 K. Thorndahl-G. Ahm (Denmark)
1952 A. Jacobsen-G. Ahm (Denmark)
1953 I. Cooley-J. White (England)
1954 S. Devlin-J. Devlin (U.S.A.)
1955 I. Cooley-J. White (England)
1956 S. Devlin-J. Devlin (U.S.A.)
1957 A. Hansen-K. Granlund (Denmark)
1958 M. Varner-H. Ward (U.S.A.-England)
1959 W. Rogers-E. Timperley (England)
1960 S. Devlin-J. Devlin (U.S.A.)
1961 G. Hashman-F. Peard (U.S.A-Ireland)
1962 G. Hashman-T. Holst-Christensen
         (U.S.A.-Denmark)
1963 G. Hashman-F. Peard (U.S.A.-Ireland)
1964 K. Jorgensen-U. Rasmussen
         (Denmark)
1965 K. Jorgensen-U. Strand (Denmark)
1966 G. Hashman-F. Peard (U.S.A.-Ireland)
1967 I. Rietveld-U. Strand
         (Netherlands-Denmark)
1968 Minarni-R. Koestijah (Indonesia)
1969 M. Boxall-P. Whetnall (England)
1970 M. Boxall-P. Whetnall (England)
1971 N. Takagi-H. Yuki (Japan)
1972 N. Takagi-H. Yuki (Japan)
1973 M. Aizawa-E. Takenaka (Japan)
1974 M. Beck-G. Perrin Gilks (England)
1975 M. Aizawa-E. Takenaka (Japan)
1976 G. Perrin Gilks-S. Pound Whetnall
         (England)
1977 E. Takenaka Toganoo-E. Veno (Japan)
1978 A. Tokuda-M. Takada (Japan)
1979 Verawaty-I. Wigoeno (Indonesia)
1980 J. Webster-N. Gardner Perry (England)

Mixed Doubles

1947 P. Holm-T. Olsen (Denmark)
1948 J. Skaarup-K. Thorndahl (Denmark)
1949 C. Stephens-P. Stephens (U.S.A.)
1950 P. Holm-G. Ahm (Denmark)
1951 P. Holm-G. Ahm (Denmark)
1952 P. Holm-G. Ahm (Denmark)
1953 E. Choong-J. White (Malaysia-England)
1954 J. Best-I. Cooley (England)
1955 F. Kobbero-K. Thorndahl (Denmark)
1956 A. D. Jordan-E. Timperley (England)
1957 F. Kobbero-K. Granlund (Denmark)
1958 A. D. Jordan-E. Timperley (England)
1959 P. Nielsen-I. Hansen (Denmark)
1960 F. Kobbero-K. Granlund (Denmark)
1961 F. Kobbero-K. Granlund (Denmark)
1962 F. Kobbero-U. Rasmussen (Denmark)
1963 F. Kobbero-U. Rasmussen (Denmark)
1964 A. D. Jordan-J. Pritchard (England)
1965 F. Kobbero-U. Strand (Denmark)
1966 F. Kobbero-U. Strand (Denmark)
1967 S. Andersen-U. Strand (Denmark)
1968 A. D. Jordan-S. Pound (England)
1969 R. Mills-G. Perrin (England)
1970 P. Walsoe-P. Hansen (Denmark)
1971 S. Pri-U. Strand (Denmark)
1972 S. Pri-U. Strand (Denmark)
1973 D. Talbot-G. Perrin Gilks (England)
1974 D. Eddy-S. Pound Whetnall (England)
1975 E. Stuart-N. Gardner (England)
1976 D. Talbot-G. Perrin Gilks (England)
1977 D. Talbot-G. Perrin Gilks (England)
1978 M. Tredgett-N. Gardner Perry (England)
1979 Christian-I. Wigodeno (Indonesia)
1980 M. Tredgett-N. Gardner Perry (England)

THOMAS CUP CHAMPIONS (MEN)

The Thomas Cup was donated by Sir George Thomas and international team competition for men was started in 1948 and is held every three years.

Contests	Champion Nation	Runner-up
1948–49	Malaysia	Denmark
1951–52	Malaysia	U.S.A.
1954–55	Malaysia	Denmark
1957–58	Indonesia	Malaysia
1960–61	Indonesia	Thailand
1963–64	Indonesia	Denmark
1966–67	Malaysia	Indonesia
1969–70	Indonesia	Malaysia
1972–73	Indonesia	Denmark
1975–76	Indonesia	Malaysia
1978–79	Indonesia	Denmark

UBER CUP CHAMPIONS (WOMEN)

The Uber Cup was donated by Mrs. H. S. Uber and international team competition for women was started in 1956 and is held every three years.

Contests	Champion Nation	Runner-up
1956–57	U.S.A.	Denmark
1959–60	U.S.A.	Denmark
1962–63	U.S.A.	England
1965–66	Japan	U.S.A.
1968–69	Japan	Indonesia
1971–72	Japan	Indonesia
1974–75	Indonesia	Japan
1977–78	Japan	Indonesia

As can be seen by the above results, the U.S.A. has not won the Thomas Cup but has won the Uber Cup on three occasions. The Far East countries of Japan, Indonesia, and Malaysia have dominated the Thomas Cup and Uber Cup results since 1963. It is also interesting to note that badminton is the national sport of these countries along with soccer.

SUGGESTED READINGS

SUGGESTED READINGS

BOOKS

Bloss, Margaret, and Virginia Brown. *Badminton*. Dubuque, Iowa: Wm. C. Brown Co.

Davidson, Kenneth, and Leland Gustavson. *Winning Badminton*. New York: The Ronald Press Co., 1953.

Davis, Pat. *Badminton Complete*. Cranbury, N. Y.: A. S. Barnes & Co., 1967.

Downey, Jake. *Better Badminton for All*. Ontario Badminton Assn., 559 Jarvis St., Toronto, Ontario, Canada M4Y2J1.

Downey, Jake. *The Singles Game — A Framework for Badminton — An Attacking Game*. Ontario Badminton Assn., 559 Jarvis St., Toronto, Ontario, Canada M4Y2J1.

Hashman, Judy Devlin. *Badminton: A Champion's Way*. London: Kaye & Ward, 1969.

Hashman, Judy and C. M. Jones. *Beginning Badminton*. Ontario Badminton Assn., 559 Jarvis St., Toronto, Ontario, Canada M4Y2J1.

Rogers, Wynn. *Advanced Badminton*. Dubuque, Iowa: Wm. C. Brown Co., 1971.

MAGAZINES AND PERIODICALS

Badminton Gazette, Official publication of Badminton Association of England, 81a High Street, Bromley, Kent, England.

Badminton, USA, Official publication of U. S. Badminton Assn., USBA, P. O. Box 237, Swartz Creek, MI 48473.

International Badminton Federation Handbook, Mrs. V. S. Rowan, I.B.F., 24 Winchcombe House, Winchcombe St., Cheltenham, Glouchestershire, GL52 6YB, England.

Shuttle Scuttle, Official publication of the Southern California Badminton Assn., Kelly Tibbetts, 4431 Pacific Coast Highway, Apt. L–202, Torrance, Calif., 90505.

World Badminton, Official publication of I.B.F., Mrs. V. S. Rowan, 24 Winchcombe House, Winchcombe St., Cheltenham, Glouchestershire, GL52 6YB, England.